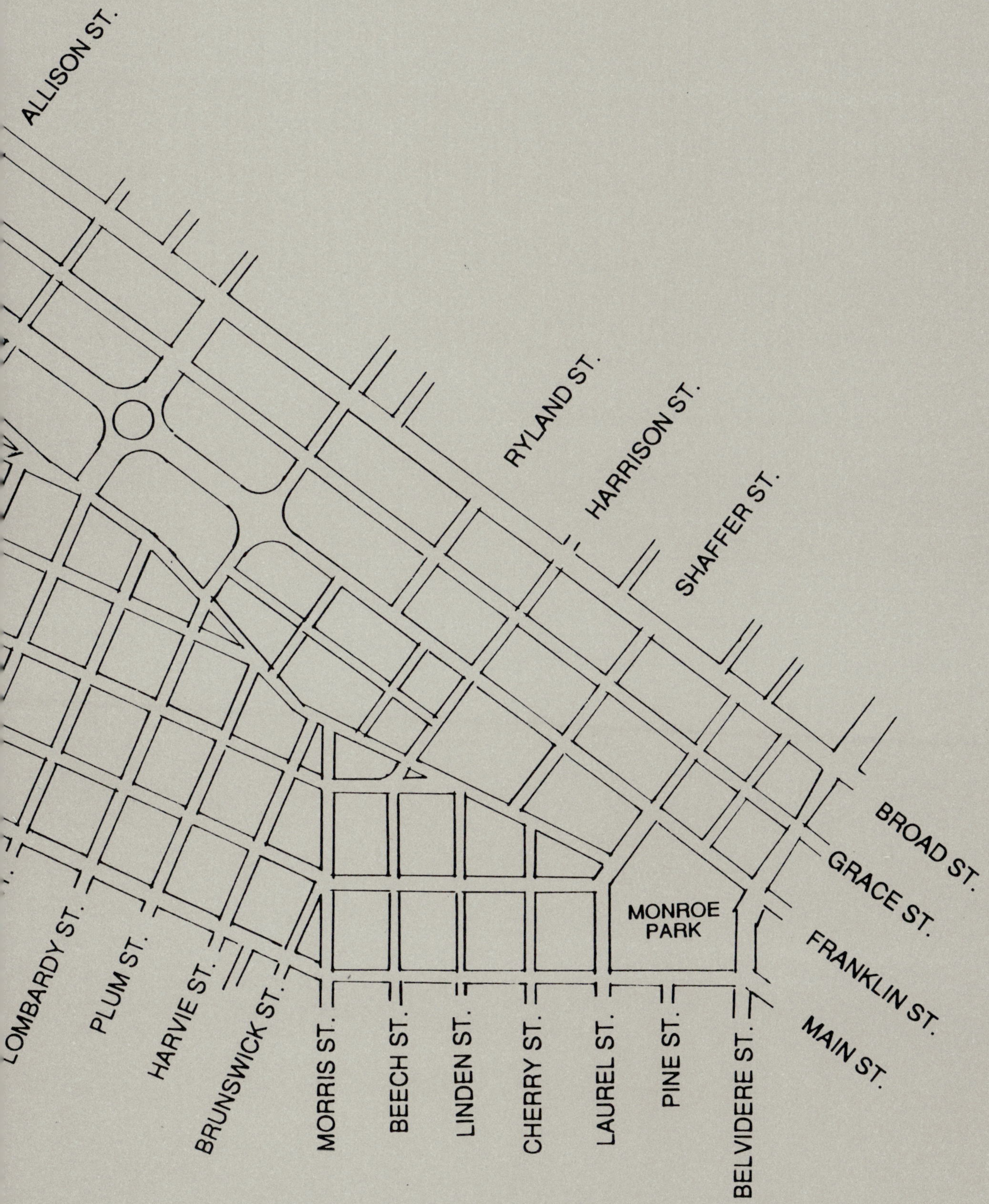
ALLISON ST.
RYLAND ST.
HARRISON ST.
SHAFFER ST.
BROAD ST.
GRACE ST.
FRANKLIN ST.
MAIN ST.
MONROE PARK
LOMBARDY ST.
PLUM ST.
HARVIE ST.
BRUNSWICK ST.
MORRIS ST.
BEECH ST.
LINDEN ST.
CHERRY ST.
LAUREL ST.
PINE ST.
BELVIDERE ST.

Richmond's Fan District

Drew St.J. Carneal

Old Dominion Row, 1500 block Grove Avenue (north side)

Color photography by Richard Cheek

Published by The Council of
Historic Richmond Foundation

To Ann
Jack and Ann Barron
thanks for your patience

Published by authority of the
Council of Historic Richmond Foundation
Library of Congress Catalog Card Number 96-77922
ISBN 1-889569-02-X

© Copyright 1996 by Historic Richmond Foundation.
This book, or portions thereof, may not be reproduced
in any form without the written approval of
Historic Richmond Foundation, Richmond, Virginia.

All rights reserved.

CONTENTS

PREFACE — 6

CHAPTER ONE The Westham Road, William Byrd III, and His Lottery, 1676–1775 — 8

CHAPTER TWO The Revolution, Scuffletown, and Its Tavern, 1775–1804 — 14

CHAPTER THREE The Mayos and Their Neighbors, 1789–1816 — 20

CHAPTER FOUR The Flush Times, 1817–1822 — 30

CHAPTER FIVE An Age of Contraction and Fear, 1819–1835 — 40

CHAPTER SIX The Canal, Railroads, and Heightened Prospects, 1836–1861 — 46

CHAPTER SEVEN The War Years, 1861–1865 — 60

CHAPTER EIGHT Annexation and Progress, 1865–1875 — 68

CHAPTER NINE "Bricks are as good as gold," 1875–1900 — 76

CHAPTER TEN "Where the shaggy corn and green turnips so lately flourished," 1900–1925 — 114

APPENDIX A Select Inventory of Streets and Houses, 1875–1900 — 150

APPENDIX B Architects, 1900–1920 — 186

APPENDIX C Builders, 1900–1920 — 198

NOTES — 212

INDEX — 231

ACKNOWLEDGMENTS — 239

CREDITS — 240

Overleaf: Plate 1 Aerial view of the Fan District looking west from Monroe Park

PREFACE

Plate 2 Doorway, 2309 Monument Avenue

This book traces the development of the Fan District, a residential neighborhood made up of late-nineteenth- and early-twentieth-century houses located several miles to the west of downtown Richmond. Its generally accepted boundaries encompass an area of more than five hundred acres extending westwardly from Monroe Park between Broad and Main Streets to the Boulevard. While the Fan District has been described as a cohesive and relatively undisturbed example of turn-of-the-century architecture, neither its current name nor its boundaries would have been recognized by those largely middle- and upper-class Richmonders who first settled there. Originally known as Sydney after a failed 1817 land promotion, the area generally was called "the west end" during its formative years. As the frontier of residential Richmond continued to move farther out to the western suburbs during the 1920s and 1930s, the area soon was left without a name. Following a twenty-year period of gradual decline experienced in the 1930s and 1940s, portions of this neighborhood underwent a rebirth in the late 1950s as the convenience of living near to the downtown as well as the charm, adaptability, and affordability of these well-built houses became apparent to growing numbers of urban aficionados and pioneers.

But when this interest was in its infancy, revitalization supporters encountered the problem that the area still had no formal name. Somehow, the generic phrase "in town" or "the town-house area" had no distinctive ring. In 1936, R. B. Munford Jr., in his *Richmond Homes and Memories*, possibly dropped a seed when he described Floyd, Grove, and Park Avenues: "which as they went further to the west, were to fan out, giving spaces for various little triangular parks from which other still newer avenues were to take their start, like slips grafted to a parent stem." Older residents began to speak of a neighborhood that "fanned out" and this sobriquet sparked the imagination of a young realtor, Neville Johnson, who in the early 1950s published a widely distributed promotional brochure that was prophetically titled "The Fan—Town Houses for Gracious Living." Buoyed by this identification, other neighborhood stalwarts began very consciously and very pointedly to refer to the area as "The Fan District." James Jackson Kilpatrick, who lived on Hanover Avenue, used his position as editor of the *Richmond News Leader* further to popularize the name by writing editorials citing the charm and the political potential of the area.

The boundaries of the Fan District were originally neither as expansive nor as precise as they now are. When the name first appeared, few knew exactly where the Fan began or ended. The task of defining this neighborhood was made more difficult by the fact that many houses found west of the Boulevard and south of Main Street were identical in date and architectural type to those later houses lying within the Fan District. But this process of creating a neighborhood was not aimed at preserving a period historic district but rather at encouraging renovation and promoting a distinct sense of community in this older section of Richmond. Led primarily by the Fan District Association, the boundaries of the Fan have over the years been expanded until they finally met the formidable traffic barriers of Main and Broad Streets and the Boulevard. Monument Avenue and Grace Street did not officially become part of the Fan District until the 1970s. Now other improvement organizations have sprung up in those adjoining areas that share a common heritage with the Fan District, and they too have been successful in developing their own identities and unique neighborhood qualities.

The first portion of this book tells the story of the Fan District area prior to its evolution as a densely built up and populated urban neighborhood. While this land remained mostly vacant until the 1880s, its history, not unlike that of other areas that once fringed small but growing cities, mirrors the long journey of the city of Richmond from a small frontier trading post to one of the leading cities of the South. First cleared for the cultivation of tobacco, which was shipped from the small colonial port at Rocketts, the land then became traversed by several roads used for trade between Richmond and Virginia's western frontier. Included in William Byrd III's 1769 lottery of most of his holdings in Richmond, this acreage experienced the brief appearance of a small roadside community known as Scuffletown, which was linked to Richmond's developing coal industry. It soon attracted a few of the city's wealthier citizens who erected substantial suburban estates, as well as three Richmond speculators who lost their fortunes in an 1817 land scheme known as the Town of Sydney. During the several decades preceding the Civil War, a number of the city's middle-class merchants and businessmen commenced building small cottage retreats. The war, however, brought a protracted period of economic devastation to Richmond, and it was not until the 1880s that the area began its final transformation into a new and modern neighborhood in a thriving city.

Individual attention may be given to most of the Fan District houses built before 1900 as their numbers were relatively few; however, singular treatment of the hundreds of houses erected after the turn of the century would fill several volumes as well as exhaust the body and mind of the most diligent researcher. Therefore, in the later chapters of this book, these post-1900 houses are generally treated either as examples of architectural styles or as the products of particular architects or builders. This approach unfortunately slights many dwellings of architectural merit but in time these houses should be given the attention they deserve in other works of more particularized scope than this.

Focusing mainly on the physical and architectural development of the Fan District, this book only hints at the social history of the people who lived in its houses. Memoirs and anecdotes of these families—some of which detail several generations of Fan District life—are left for others to write. As the Fan District was built primarily by white middle- and upper-income people for people of like condition, the contributions of Richmond's numerous ethnic and racial minorities to the societal life-force of this neighborhood also are left unrecorded here. Although members of Richmond's African American community provided much of the skilled labor to build the Fan District and render many of the exacting services required by white families to function comfortably, the participation of African Americans as property owners or economic stakeholders in the development of the area was totally precluded by the dehumanizing prejudices and practices of the times.

Finally, I express my apologies for any errors or omissions that may come to light after the publication of this book. My research began many years ago when I had no idea that my hastily scribbled notes on hundreds of houses, events, and personages would one day be transformed into a volume offered to the public. I hope that any errors are of minor importance and that they will find correction in an appropriate and timely manner.

Drew St.J. Carneal

CHAPTER ONE

The Westham Road, William Byrd III, and His Lottery

1676–1775

In 1773 an English visitor departed from the small town of Richmond and rode west to an even smaller settlement known as Westham. There he duly reported on the unloading of hogsheads of tobacco that had been rafted down the James River from the backcountry.[1] To accomplish this seven-mile trip, our Englishman traveled a narrow country road that left the tobacco warehouses clustered around Shockoe Creek, traversed a steep hill, and then snaked its way westward through the undulating Virginia countryside where many years later Richmond's Fan District and West End neighborhoods would appear.[2]

Originating most probably as an Indian trail joining upland and Tidewater tribes, the Westham Road had from an early date played a vital part in the history of the Virginia colony (fig. 1). Agents dispatched by the merchants at the falls to trade with the Indians returned down the Westham Road with valuable loads of bear, deer, beaver, and other native furs that were especially treasured by the European markets. As the western lands became settled and cultivated, tobacco and grains replaced animal hides as the main staples of trade, and water transportation became essential to convey these heavy crops to market. Because the James River was navigable from the west only to the head of the falls—about seven miles above the port of Richmond—produce and commodities were rafted downstream, unloaded at the wharves of Westham, and then carted overland around the falls to Richmond via the Westham Road. Rather than closely paralleling the banks of the James, the road's path was forced inland by the deep ravines and small creeks bordering the river to seek a relatively flat plateau to the north where the transport of heavily ladened wagons and carts was less difficult.

Much of the terrain through which the Westham

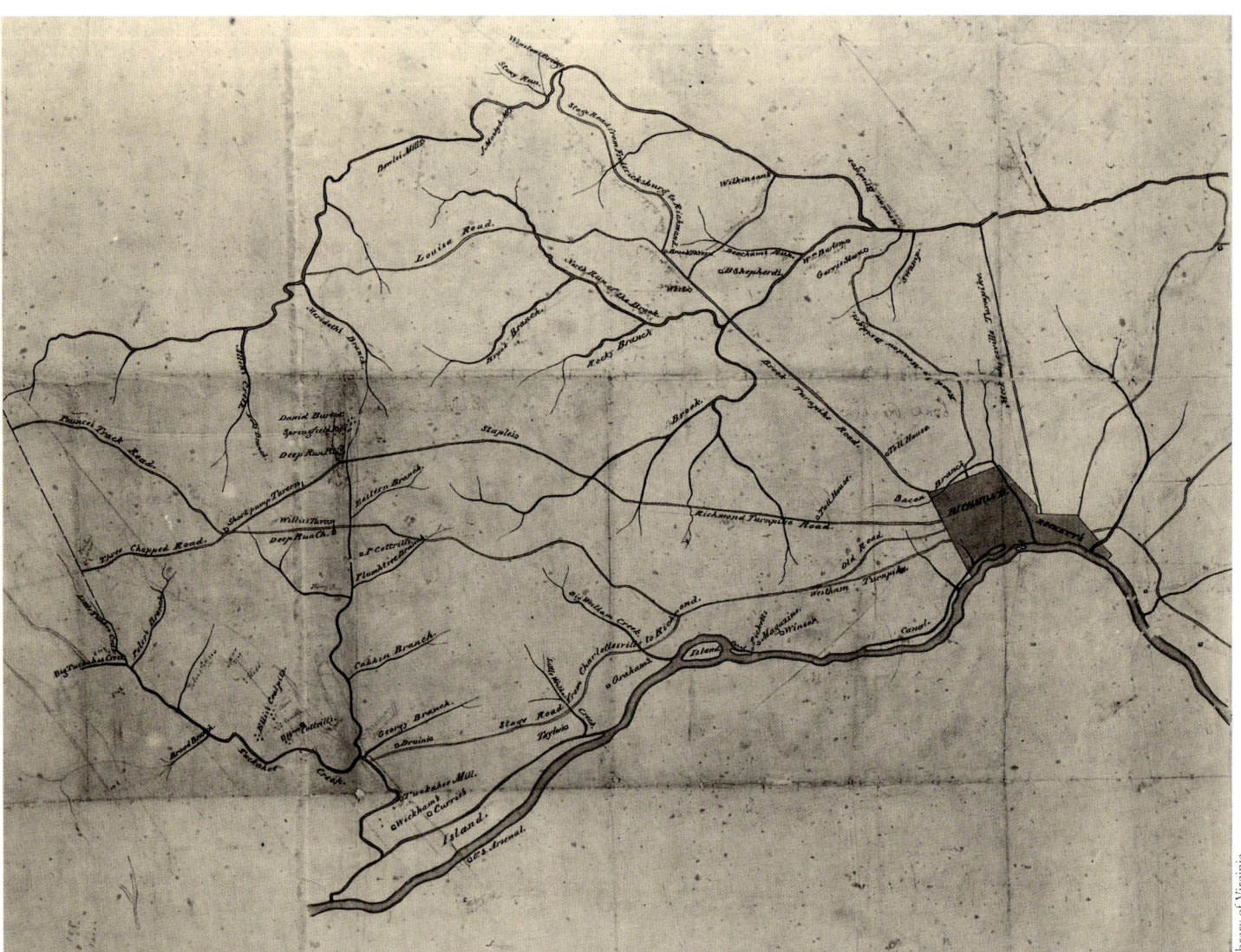

Fig. 1 Depicted as the "Old Road" on this ca.1819 map of Henrico County, the Westham Road was the main route from Richmond to the west prior to the construction of the Richmond Turnpike Road and Westham Turnpike.

Plate 3 William Byrd III (1728–1777)

Road passed had been included in a sizable land grant made about 1676 to William Byrd I.[3] Byrd had immigrated to Virginia prior to 1670 to work at the trading post of his uncle, Thomas Stegge Jr., at the fall line of the James River. Upon Stegge's death, Byrd inherited his uncle's holdings and energetically expanded them into a diverse and profitable commercial enterprise. At his death in 1704, the tract passed to his son William Byrd II, the "Black Swan" of Westover and the founder of the town of Richmond,[4] and then in 1744 to his son William Byrd III (plate 3). During the long years of this Byrd fiefdom, trees were cleared from the land, fields were opened, and crops were sown and reaped in seemingly endless regularity.

By 1756, William Byrd III had laid an avenue off the Westham Road about a mile west of Richmond and built a large house, Belvidere, that overlooked the river.[5] The grandeur of Belvidere obviously lay in its setting; a terraced lawn sloped to the rocky turbulence of the falls below, and downstream the small town of Richmond could be seen nestled serenely on the riverbank. As described in several later fire insurance policies and Benjamin Henry Latrobe's watercolor (plate 4), Belvidere was an imposing two-story frame structure measuring more than one hundred thirty feet in length and flanked on the east by an office and on the west by a kitchen.[6]

William Byrd III's stake in the economic health and growth of the town of Richmond was substantial as he still controlled most of its commerce as well as much of its land.[7] Byrd, however, did not have the inclination to promote the trade and manufacturing potential of Richmond; shortly after Belvidere's construction in mid-1756, it was reported in a letter to George Washington that Byrd had "repudiated his Wife, who is now in a Delirium for his Behaviour, and is Resolved to make a Campaign under Lord Loudon—he has committed his Estate to the Charge of Some Friends, & Settled all with a design never to return to Virginia."[8] Byrd's real passion was military adventure, and he joined the commander in chief of the British forces in America, John Campbell, earl of Loudoun, in the French and Indian War, while Belvidere became the retreat of the "repudiated" wife, Elizabeth Hill Carter.[9] Granddaughter of the imperious Robert "King" Carter of Corotoman, Elizabeth Byrd had borne five children in seven years of marriage and now at age thirty, she found Belvidere a place where "I am affraid my youth & life will be buried in retirement and dissatisfaction."[10] On 25 July 1760, she died at Belvidere under mysterious circumstances—it was rumored that she had turned a large chest over on herself.[11] Six months later, Byrd married Mary Willing whose father had been mayor of Philadelphia. It was not until the autumn of 1762 that Byrd returned to Virginia, where he shortly made Westover rather than Belvidere his principal place of residence.

During his long absence from Virginia, Byrd's

Plate 4 Watercolor of Belvidere painted by B. H. Latrobe in 1797

financial situation had grown steadily worse. While his family estate still controlled huge tracts of land together with various business enterprises and hundreds of slaves, the carrying expenses of these properties combined with Byrd's proclivity to spend beyond his means left him short of both cash and credit. Byrd was able to win a few years of peace by persuading the omnipotent treasurer of the colony, John Robinson, to include him among the coterie of Tidewater aristocrats to whom Robinson was making illegal loans out of the public treasury. Robinson's untimely death in 1766, however, exposed these peculations and left Byrd holding the largest single amount of the loans.[12] He again faced an involuntary liquidation of his patrimony that would be made at great sacrifice unless executed in at least an orderly and timely fashion.

In pondering his dilemma, Byrd and his trustees decided on a bold course of action—he would place on the market all of his family's extensive holdings at the falls. The Byrd estate in the Richmond area included commercial interests, river islands, tenements and lots in Richmond itself, and also Rocky Ridge (located directly across the James and formally named the town of Manchester in 1769), as well as larger tracts of land surrounding both towns. His marketing plan was equally bold—he would offer to the public 10,000 chances for these holdings at £5 per chance. If all went as scheduled, the tickets would be drawn in June 1768 and there would be 839 winners. Thus, the lottery was duly advertised in the *Virginia Gazette* and Byrd optimistically undertook the organization and promotion of the enormous venture.[13]

Packets of numbered tickets (plate 5) were printed and distributed to Byrd's friends and associates for sale throughout the colonies and also across the sea in England. In April 1768 Thomas Adams wrote Byrd from London that he still hoped to dispose of all his tickets there to "tradesmen of note" before the drawing.[14] When a ticket was sold, its stub was to be returned to one of the managers for safekeeping, but disappointing returns dictated that the drawing be postponed from June until November 1768 and its location changed from Richmond to Williamsburg. Byrd and presumably all of his managers finally did gather in Williamsburg where they duly performed the historic drawing; it is apparent, however, that far less than £50,000 was on hand when the names of the "fortunate adventurers," as the winners became known, were announced.[15] The following year the General Assembly, troubled by the absence of regulations surrounding these schemes, cited the "common good and welfare of the community" in outlawing all future private lotteries in the colony.[16]

One hundred of these prizes consisted of tracts of 100 acres each that radiated out to the north and west of Richmond (fig. 2). The block of western lots ran three deep from the river out as far as present-day Three Chopt Road. The path of the Westham Road was used as the boundary line between the second and third tiers. The task of laying off one hundred lots of 100 acres each would have been a difficult and time-consuming assignment under relatively normal circumstances and the added challenge of fitting these lots within the gullied banks of a falling river and a meandering country road would have tested the skill of the most competent surveyor in the colony. While a more-detailed plat of the lots than shown on the plat of prize lots was lodged for inspection at the Henrico County courthouse, whether Byrd's surveyor, Benjamin Watkins of Chesterfield County,[17] made an accurate plat of each lot is doubtful; he probably set some corner pins and then left the job of determining exactly where the lines should run to the later agreement or disagreement of the abutting fortunate adventurers.

In the area that many years later would become known as the near West End and still later the Fan District of Richmond, the fortunate adventurers or early owners of the 100-acre lots as shown on the plat of prize lots were John Pleasants (lot 803), Daniel Price (lots 758, 759, 760, and the unnumbered lot on the north), Alexander McCaul (lots 743, 754, 755, and 756), and James Buchanan (lots 795 and 796).[18] All had business interests in Richmond and all except McCaul resided in the area. McCaul was a Scottish

Plate 5 Ticket for William Byrd III's lottery of properties in Richmond

merchant whose firm, Henderson, McCaul & Company, operated a large warehouse in Manchester under the local management of James Lyle.[19] McCaul's winning tickets probably were obtained in exchange for money Byrd owed the firm.

Although he would be reappointed as a town trustee by the legislature in 1773, Byrd had lost his influence in the affairs of the colony. For the first time in more than one hundred years, a Byrd neither owned nor controlled the strategic operations at the falls. Following the drawing, an insolvent Byrd retreated to Westover where he petulantly undertook a largely unsuccessful effort to collect on those losing lottery tickets that had been bought on credit before the drawing. Later when relations between Virginia and England became strained, Byrd refused to declare his loyalty to either side and his ambivalence earned him the enmity and abuse of his countrymen. Beset by these and other problems,[20] Byrd saw the new year of 1777 come in at Westover and then later that day committed suicide. He was forty-eight years old.

The results of the lottery did not have an immediate effect on the town of Richmond or its environs; the few income-producing prizes were promptly spoken for; most of the four hundred unimproved half-acre lots lying to the west of Shockoe Creek, however, proved to be inaccessible. They were therefore neither usable nor marketable, as the grid pattern of streets so conveniently and neatly shown on the lottery plat had not yet been laid over the formidable hills and gullies of this envisioned new section of town. Even the outlying lots of one hundred acres were of little value; after years of growing the soil-enervating crop of tobacco, these "Old Fields," as they were rather derisively called, could no longer support profitable agricultural activities and were considered fit only for random foraging by livestock.

Accordingly, even after whatever public commotion the lottery had provoked had died down, the town remained very much as it had been before the drawing—a relatively small but energetic river port containing the usual complement of wooden warehouses, stores, and taverns clustered along the banks of the James—except that now the town and surrounding tracts were no longer owned by a Byrd. In the spring of 1771 many of these buildings were devastated by a flood of unprecedented magnitude that abruptly checked all commercial activity. For the next few years Richmond was preoccupied with rebuilding its economic base. While the townspeople went about this task, delegates to the second revolutionary convention gathered in March 1775 at Saint John's Church on Church Hill to air their grievances with colonial rule. The ensuing hostilities with Great Britain would move this small community toward an unexpected destiny.

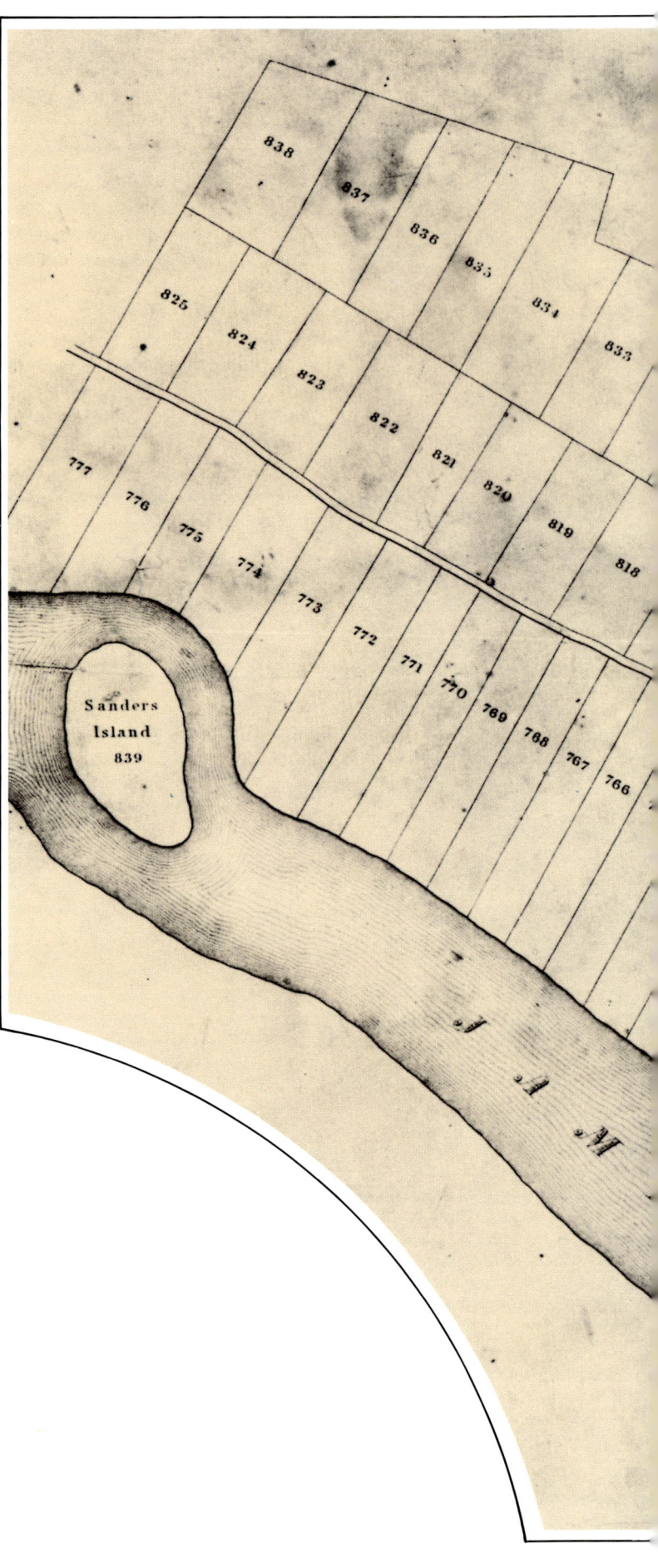

Chapter One

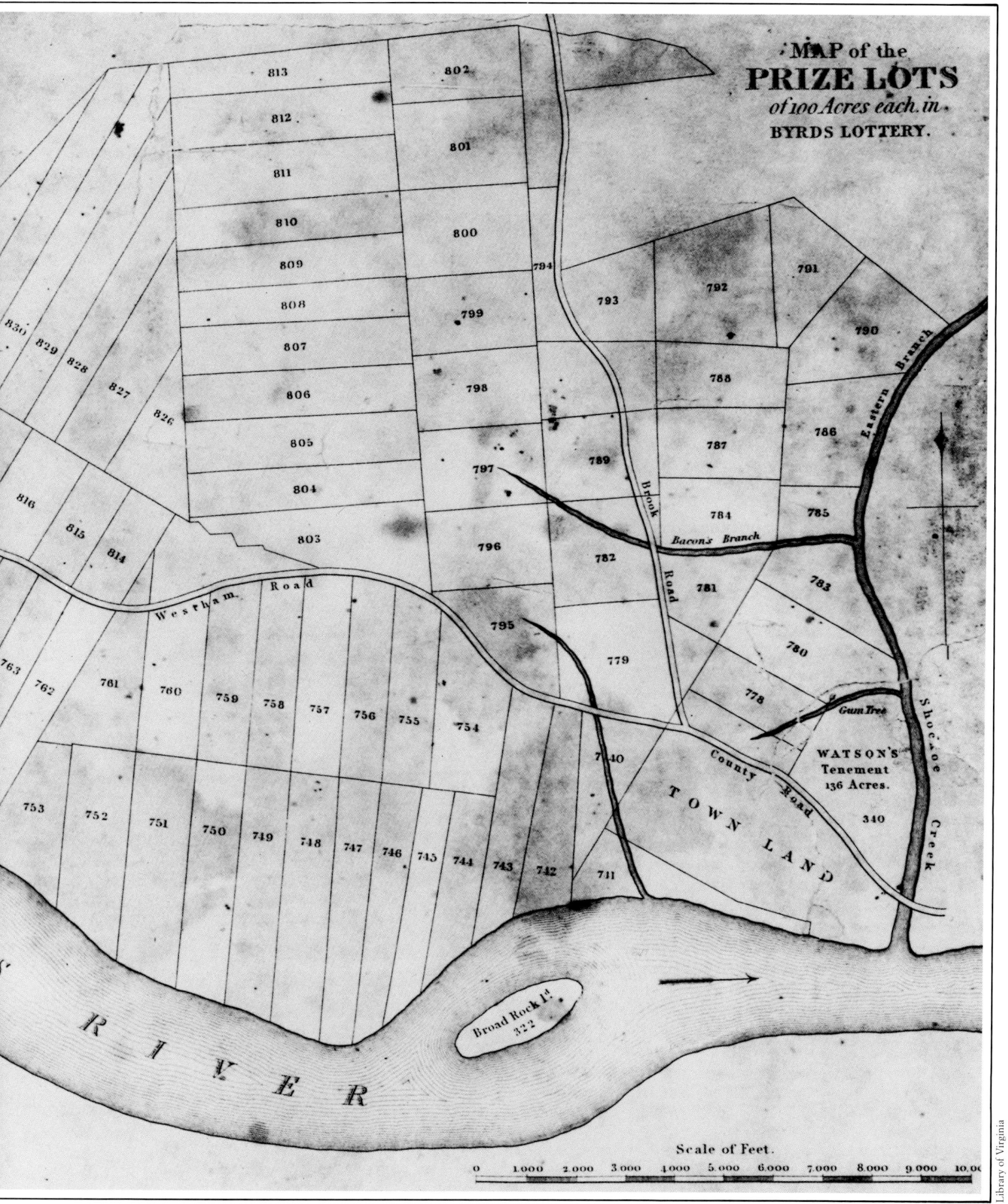

Fig. 2 The 1769 Lottery of the lands and properties of William Byrd III contained much of Richmond's present Northside and West End neighborhoods including the entire Fan District. (Map of the City of Richmond by Micajah Bates, 1835)

CHAPTER TWO

The Revolution, Scuffletown, and Its Tavern

1775–1804

The coming of revolution to the North American colonies had spanned the years from the end of the French and Indian War in 1763 until the colonists at Lexington and Concord, Massachusetts, fired in April 1775 "the shot heard round the world." Whatever Richmonders may have felt about being part of the British Empire, the Virginia colony had been moving in the direction of independence since the Stamp Acts of 1766. After the royal governor, John Murray, earl of Dunmore, prorogued the House of Burgesses in May 1774, Virginia's first revolutionary convention met 1–6 August 1774 to choose delegates to the First Continental Congress, where the issue of seeking independence from Great Britain would be debated and decided.

By the time Virginia's second revolutionary convention met in 1775, hostilities had already broken out in Massachusetts. The convention moved to defend Virginia against British invasion by formally authorizing the arming of the militia in each county. With lower Tidewater Virginia particularly vulnerable to enemy attack from the rivers and estuaries of the Chesapeake Bay, the area lying about the falls of the James River was looked on as a secure place to prepare for a war that most expected would be of limited duration. By the end of 1778, Virginia had commissioned the building of a foundry, boring mill, and magazine at a site along the river located just off the Westham Road about five miles west of the town. There, using a short canal dug for the operation, coal from the Deep Run pits located in the western part of the county[1] and ore rafted down the river from the backcountry were converted to iron and cast into cannon and shot. Although the operation was referred to as the Westham Foundry, it actually was located about a mile downriver from the Westham portage. In addition, the relocation there of the State Laboratory, which was primarily responsible for arms repair and the manufacture of cartridges, added to the growing military importance of this area.

As the war escalated and moved south, the General Assembly decreed in 1779 that "the seat of government [be relocated] to the town of Richmond, in the county of Henrico, which is more safe and central than any other town situated on navigable water." Accordingly, in April 1780 the accoutrements of government were transported from Williamsburg to Richmond, joining the store of public records that had already been lodged there in 1777 for safekeeping. Thomas Jefferson was the first Virginia governor to take up residence in the new capital even though no state buildings had yet been erected and the town itself was totally unprepared for its designated role as Virginia's seat of government.

The legislature's opinion that the Richmond area was secure from enemy attack was soon to be tested. Although Governor Jefferson was aware of the presence of Brigadier General Benedict Arnold's British flotilla in the lower James River during the latter part of 1780, he was surprised to learn on the morning of 4 January 1781 that the convoy was moving up the river toward Richmond. That evening, he was shocked to learn that Arnold and his forces had landed at Westover and already were advancing on Richmond. Jefferson ordered that the arms and military stores that remained in town as well the public records be taken to the foundry for safekeeping and then he himself retreated up the Westham Road to the general vicinity of Tuckahoe Creek. As the British main force occupied the town, Lieutenant Colonel John Graves Simcoe, of the Queen's Rangers, with about thirty cavalrymen and a regiment of infantry, moved out the Westham Road to the foundry where they burned and destroyed the operation and the stores found on the site. With their mission completed, that evening the Redcoats retired back down the Westham Road but not before experiencing some sort of scuffle with Virginia militiamen in the vicinity of the present intersection of Mulberry Street and Grove Avenue. What actually happened is unclear, but it is highly improbable that the reported encounter amounted to anything more than a few militiamen closely checking the British rear guard as it withdrew along the road to town. Indeed, Jefferson later admitted that the enemy attacked and left Richmond with "total impunity" and Baron Friedrich von Steuben complained that he had not heard of a single gun being fired at the enemy during its stay in Richmond. Today a marker stands at this busily traveled intersection to commemorate the "driving in of Arnold's pickets" (fig. 3).[2]

A few months later the Westham Road again experienced the tramp of soldiers' boots and the roll of military supply wagons. In June 1781 at the intersection of the Three Chopt and the Westham Roads the "Hunting Leopard," Lieutenant Colonel Banastre Tarleton, and his cavalry retiring from Charlottesville joined the army of General Charles Cornwallis, which was traveling down the river from Point of Fork in Fluvanna County. Together, the united forces marched past the ruins of the Westham Foundry and through Richmond to their fateful encampment at Yorktown.

The Coal Industry

During the war years, the Westham Road began to carry an increasing number of wagons hauling coal to Richmond from the Deep Run pits located in the western part of the county. The presence of coal deposits lying just to the west of Richmond had been known since at least the days of William Byrd I, but transportation difficulties and an indifferent market had discouraged serious exploitation.[3] The war, however, had ended the importation of foreign coal and the quality of the local fuel proved surprisingly effective in the manufacture of arms and other war matériel. As coal became widely popular for industrial and then domestic uses along the eastern seaboard, the mining and sale of the abundant deposits found in Henrico, Chesterfield, and Goochland Counties rapidly developed into a major business. Thus the coal industry provided Richmond's slack economy with a new trade commodity and, more important, a raw material that in ready and cheap supply would attract additional industries to the city.

Scuffletown and the Richmond Turnpike

As the Henrico pits lay a short distance east of the Three Chopt Road, north of the future path of Broad Street, the wagons first moved south down the Three Chopt Road to its intersection with the Westham Road and then into town. With these coal wagons and the usual Westham traffic passing by with growing regularity, an enterprising carpenter named John Pleasants[4] began about 1781 to market lots ranging from one-half to three acres along the road frontage of his Byrd Lottery Lot 803, which he had purchased from William Byrd III and his trustees in 1769.[5] It is unclear why Pleasants felt that this particular spot along the Westham Road had any development potential—possibly a nice grove of trees or a watering place provided the attraction—yet within the next two years he had found buyers for five of the lots and it appears that he had constructed houses on several before they were actually sold. Pleasants, a member of an old and distinguished Henrico family of long-professing Quakers,[6] did not erect a house there for himself. He lived on family property in the eastern part of the county where he died in 1783 after having been disowned by his White Oak Quaker meeting for "disorderly practices." It was charged that he had "been concerned in the sale of a negro, subscribed to a Test [taken an oath], and frequently taken strong drink to excess."[7]

As the market for coal continued to expand, the new owners of the Deep Run pits, David Ross and Dr. James Currie, petitioned the Henrico County Court in 1788 for a new and more direct road between the pits and Richmond, citing also the need for "Good Water for the teams of which the other Road is destitute."[8] The following year the court approved this construction. The new artery, which was called the Coalpit Road, was built to bypass much of the western stretch of the Westham Road but did rejoin it along John Pleasants's western property line for the final leg into town.[9] This new intersection, near the present-day juncture of Park Avenue and Stafford Street, spurred a modest amount of further development. Charles

Fig. 3 This marker, located at the northeast corner of Grove Avenue and Mulberry Street, commemorates the Revolutionary War skirmish between the American militia and the British forces of General Benedict Arnold that took place along the path of the Westham Road in 1781.

Chapter Two

Fig. 4 Most of the buildings of Scuffletown, including its tavern, were concentrated along a bend in the Westham Road between the present Rowland Street and Stafford Avenue, although other building lots and several other houses extended eastwardly to the present Allen Avenue.

Price, who had been given the Byrd lot to the west by his father, built a dwelling for himself "in the fork of the two ditches" close by Pleasants's line. He also staked off and sold at least four other lots running along the road.[10] Meanwhile, John Pleasants's son Tarleton successfully marketed most of the remaining road-front lots laid off by his father.

By 1791, Pleasants's and Price's former lots had become popularly known as "Scuffletown." While it is tempting to attribute the name as descriptive of the activities emanating from a tavern and some race paths that came to be located in this small settlement, it appears more likely that "Scuffletown" was coined to commemorate the 1781 skirmish or "scuffle" that had taken place between the Virginia militia and Benedict Arnold's pickets a short distance up the road.[11] Even though some of Pleasants's and Price's lots were assigned numbers in their deeds, thereby implying a plan of development, there is no record that Scuffletown was ever officially sanctioned as a town by the legislature. Yet by 1795 about one dozen structures dotted the north side of the Westham Road in an area that today would extend along Park Avenue from a spot generally opposite Rowland Street out to beyond Stafford Avenue (fig. 4). As all of the structures except one disappeared over a relatively short period of time and without lasting comment, it must be assumed that the buildings of Scuffletown were plain wooden affairs—attended with the usual rural complex of stables, smokehouses, and in some cases a servant's cabin—reflecting the modest incomes that could be derived from farming the nearby fields or providing services to the commerce of the road.

The only Scuffletown building that has left any social or pictorial history is a roadside tavern (fig. 5) about which it was recollected in 1845:

> The race course was at Scuffle Town where a tavern was kept; the sign represented the world with a man's head and shoulders emerging from the orb, and crying "help a scuffler through."[12]

Some years later the sagacious Richmond chronicler Samuel Mordecai embellished this Scuffletown story:

> The original settler kept a tavern there, with the anciently used sign of a globe, the head of the proprietor protruding at the north and his feet at the south pole, with the legend, "Help a *scuffler* through the world."[13]

This tavern was in operation at least by 6 November 1792, as on that date William Collins was granted a license by the Henrico County Court "to keep an ordinary at his house situate at Scuffle Town," and in 1794 he renewed his license for another year.[14] Little else is known about William Collins except that he erected the tavern building in 1791 or 1792 on a half-acre lot and within a few years he mortgaged the following possessions found in or about his tavern:

One old Negro man named Job, seven feather beds and furniture, 2 eight day clocks, 1 chest of draws, 3 dining tables of walnut and pine, 1 sorrel mare, cart and gear, 1 dray, a weading [sic] hoe and 3 grubbing [hoes], 1 set of blacksmith's tools, 1 woman's saddle and bridle, 1 man's saddle and pad, 1 shuffleboard and weights, 3 large trunks and 1 small [trunk], 5 looking glases [sic] and other household and kitchen furniture.[15]

A scrutiny of this inventory provides insight into the nature and the variety of services offered by Collins. Meals obviously were served at the dining tables, and the shuffleboard with weights suggests that some customers stopped by for a convivial round of wine, toddy, or beer. Those who slept in the featherbeds did not tarry long enough to unpack their belongings and therefore one chest of drawers was sufficient; instead, baggage and valuables were secured in one of the four trunks found on the premises. In the mornings and at mealtimes the five mirrors, probably hung side by side in a lavatory area, saw heavy duty. The chiming of the two clocks proclaimed the breakfast, dinner, and supper hours, as well as checkout times, and thus enabled the patrons to set off promptly for their scheduled appointments. With his dray and set of blacksmith's tools, Collins could provide for the repair of disabled wagons along the road, the shoeing of horses, and other services of a light mechanical nature. For transportation, Collins and presumably his wife saddled up the sorrel mare for individual sojourns. The cart was used for family trips to town or to social events as well as for the hauling of necessary supplies. Job probably served as the general handyman of the establishment, performing many of the various duties required by the tavern's operations.

Around 1800 Collins lost the tavern through foreclosure and in 1803 it was bought by Elisha Williams, who owned the lot next door.[16] It is possible that the tavern was kept open during this time but it seems more likely that Williams, his wife, Phoebe, and their eight children made the building their home.[17] When Williams died in 1806, he was buried in a small brick enclosure behind the tavern where later his wife was also interred. Both would lie in Scuffletown until 1878

Fig. 5a The southern front of the Scuffletown Tavern that faced the Westham Road

Chapter Two

when the relocation of Park Avenue necessitated the removal of their remains for reburial in Hollywood Cemetery.[18]

The Richmond Turnpike

Attesting to the sustained vigor of the coal market, early in 1804 Ross and Currie, now deeming the Coalpit and Westham Roads unsatisfactory for their needs, petitioned the legislature for "the establishment of a turnpike road the most direct way from the City of Richmond to the Deep run Coal pits" in order to "facilitate the transportation of that valuable article coal and add to the accommodation of travellers by affording them at all times a good road."[19] Accordingly, the Richmond Turnpike Company was authorized by an act of assembly passed on 5 January 1804 to open, improve, and keep in repair a turnpike road "at least forty feet wide, with a sufficient ditch on each side, and well covered with gravel or stone, so as to render the passing of waggons thereon as convenient as possible, without being paved." This new turnpike bypassed Scuffletown completely and followed a course now represented by West Broad Street. Several weeks later the legislature also created the Richmond and Columbia Turnpike Company to lay and construct a road "from the end of Main Street in the City of Richmond by the most convenient route to Goochland Court House." This turnpike would eventually be developed into the Westham Plank Road, now West Cary Street and Cary Street Road.

The opening of these roads and the successful circumnavigation of the falls by the newly constructed James River Canal, which was a going concern by 1795, sounded the death knell for Scuffletown. As the traffic on the Westham and Coalpit Roads diminished, Scuffletown languished and its townspeople gradually moved on to seek new fortunes elsewhere. Their small properties were sold to adjoining landowners or abandoned to the fortunes of the elements. During the first quarter of the new century the village quietly died away and became largely forgotten; only the sturdy tavern building and a few family burial plots remained of what had once been the small community of Scuffletown.

Fig. 5b The dirt tracings of Park Avenue can be seen in the foreground of this ca. 1880 photograph of the northern (rear) side of the Scuffletown Tavern and its outbuildings.

CHAPTER THREE

The Mayos and Their Neighbors

1789–1816

By 1789, an enterprising Richmonder, John Mayo Jr. (fig. 6a), began to use the Westham Road to commute from his suburban home, which he had named the Hermitage, to his place of business in the city. Lying just to the north of Scuffletown near the present-day Broad Street Station–Science Museum of Virginia complex,[1] the Hermitage estate, composed of six of the hundred-acre Byrd lottery lots, had been given to Mayo by his father in 1781.[2] Within the next few years Mayo and his bride, Abigail DeHart (fig. 6b), of Elizabeth, New Jersey, had moved there from a brick structure on Council Chamber Hill in time for the 1789 birth of their first child, Maria (fig. 6c).

Unlike William Byrd III, John Mayo devoted his energies to the development of the commercial potential of Richmond, a vision that was instilled in him by his father. John Mayo Sr., son of the William Mayo who had laid out the original 1737 town plan of Richmond for William Byrd II, had built up important commercial interests in the town of Manchester.[3] Frustrated by the unreliable ferry service across the river, in 1784 he obtained the approval of the legislature to build a private toll bridge joining Richmond and Manchester. John Mayo Jr. took up his father's project on the latter's death in 1786 and purchased a river island that gave him the necessary access for a north shore abutment.[4] Despite "the despair of his friends and the ridicule of his opponents"—he reportedly was jailed for his debts—Mayo realized his dream in 1788. The bridge, even though it was crude and required constant repair, proved to be a financial bonanza and the twenty-eight-year-old Mayo began prudently investing his profits in mills, manufactories, and real estate in and about Richmond.[5]

It seems likely that the Mayos first resided in the small cottage shown in the foreground of the 1797 Latrobe watercolor (fig. 7) and then added the larger brick structure to accommodate their growing family.[6] While far more substantial than the modest frame houses of Scuffletown, Mayo's Hermitage was by no means grand or pretentious. The two-story brick main building measured only thirty-two by twenty-three feet, but it did ramble on back, with a two-story enclosed porch connecting it to the one-story, thirty-two-by-eighteen-foot frame cottage (fig. 8).[7] As its name implies, the Hermitage looked out on a pastoral setting; to the south the buildings of Scuffletown might barely be seen across the fields and to the north the house commanded a vista of the Bacon's Quarter Branch[8] as it cut a course to its downstream junction with Shockoe Creek.

Mayo's decision to commute from a country house to his place of business in the city went against

Fig. 6a Colonel John Mayo Jr. (1760–1818) of the Hermitage and Bellville

Fig. 6b Abigail DeHart Mayo (1761–1843)

Fig. 6c Maria Mayo (1789–1862), daughter of Colonel John and Abigail Mayo, was married at Bellville in 1817 to Winfield Scott, a hero of the War of 1812 and later commanding general of the U.S. Army under President Abraham Lincoln.

Fig. 7 Watercolor of the Hermitage painted by B. H. Latrobe in 1797

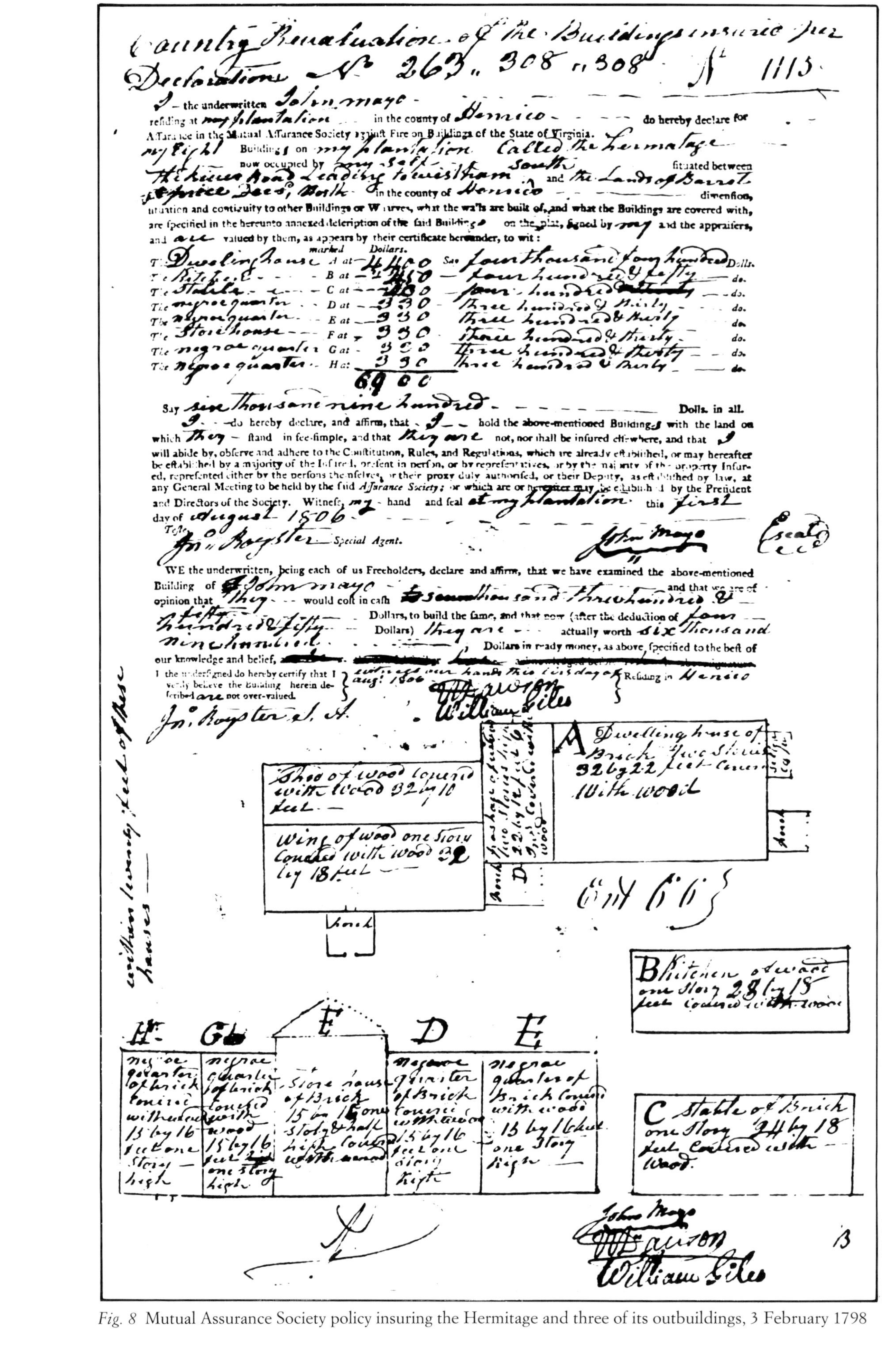

Country Revaluation of the Buildings insured per Declarations № 263. 308 . 308 № 1115

I the underwritten John Mayo residing at my plantation in the county of Henrico do hereby declare for Assurance in the Mutual Assurance Society against Fire on Buildings of the State of Virginia, my eight Buildings on my plantation called the Hermitage now occupied by my self situated between the Road Leading to Westham South and the Lands of Barrot & Price Decs^d. North in the county of Henrico the dimension, situation and contiguity to other Buildings or Wharves, what the walls are built of, and what the Buildings are covered with, are specified in the hereunto annexed description of the said Buildings on the plat, signed by me and the appraisers, and are valued by them, as appears by their certificate hereunder, to wit:

	marked	Dollars.	Say	
The Dwelling house	A at	4400	four thousand four hundred	Dolls.
The Kitchen	B at	450	four hundred & fifty	do.
The Stable	C at	300	four hundred	do.
The negroe quarter	D at	330	three hundred & thirty	do.
The negroe quarter	E at	330	three hundred & thirty	do.
The Storehouse	F at	330	three hundred & thirty	do.
The negroe quarter	G at	330	three hundred & thirty	do.
The negroe quarter	H at	330	three hundred & thirty	do.
		6900		

Say six thousand nine hundred Dolls. in all.

I do hereby declare, and affirm, that I hold the above-mentioned Buildings with the land on which they stand in fee-simple, and that they are not, nor shall be insured elsewhere, and that I will abide by, observe and adhere to the Constitution, Rules, and Regulations, which are already established, or may hereafter be established by a majority of the Insured, present in person, or by representatives, or by the majority of the property Insured, represented either by the persons themselves, or their proxy duly authorised, or their Deputy, as established by law, at any General Meeting to be held by the said Assurance Society; or which are or hereafter may be established by the President and Directors of the Society. Witness my hand and seal at my plantation this first day of August 1806

Teste
Jno. Royster Special Agent. — John Mayo (Seal)

WE the underwritten, being each of us Freeholders, declare and affirm, that we have examined the above-mentioned Building of John Mayo and that we are of opinion that they would cost in cash seven thousand three hundred & fifty Dollars, to build the same, and that now (after the deduction of four hundred & fifty Dollars) they are actually worth six thousand nine hundred Dollars in ready money, as above specified to the best of our knowledge and belief, witness our hands this 1st day of Augt 1806 — Residing in Henrico

I the undersigned do hereby certify that I verily believe the Building herein described are not over-valued.
Jno. Royster S. A. — W^m. Mayo [?] — William Giles

Fig. 8 Mutual Assurance Society policy insuring the Hermitage and three of its outbuildings, 3 February 1798

the conventional wisdom, practiced so faithfully by the Scottish merchants, that one should live within or close by his business establishment. Mayo saw these fields as a place where he and his family could flee the congestion and illnesses of a growing city and also retain some of the values and amenities of the older way of life into which he had been born. John Mayo's daybook for the period May 1800–August 1801 gives a glimpse of the pleasant moments that he experienced at home on the outskirts of the city—grafting pear trees and sowing oats in the meadows that surrounded the house, burning bricks in his private kiln, slaughtering hogs after the first frost, cutting ice to replenish the icehouse supply, riding in his sleigh with his children through the snow-covered landscape, and entertaining the ladies and gentlemen of Richmond society at afternoon tea and ice cream parties, often enlivened by the flute or clarinet of local musician London Briggs.[9] John Wickham, Mayo's trusted and often-retained lawyer, wealthy miller Joseph Gallego, and Governor and Mrs. John Page were frequent guests from town. In January, the family packed up and moved to the brick town house that had once served as the chambers of the Council of State during the Revolution and then, after moving back to the Hermitage in the spring, they traveled to Mrs. Mayo's hometown in New Jersey for summer vacations in a house that Mayo had bought there most likely at his wife's urging.[10]

Mayo's suburban lifestyle was indicative of the new influences that, following the relocation of the capital to Richmond, were changing the city's established social patterns. The well-educated bureaucrats and politicians, along with a coterie of remarkably able lawyers who were attracted to the new capital, had different values and tastes from those of the tight-fisted merchants of the city. These middle-class newcomers were not content to reside in the cramped tenement district along the river. In 1790, most Richmonders still lived in an area extending for a number of blocks east and a few blocks west of Shockoe Creek, near which stood the public market, warehouses, taverns, shops, lumberyards, stables, and other business establishments. Within a few years, sufficient new wealth was being generated in Richmond to enable its growing population to establish new residential enclaves within the city. Many citizens sought housing on Richmond (Church) Hill, some were drawn to the green elevation of Shockoe (Capitol) Hill, and a few lived still farther out in newly laid off subdivisions, called "Additions," situated in the northwestern parts of town.[11] The more prosperous began to design their houses for more than utilitarian purposes and the concept of style in architecture and interior design became manifest in a number of these new Richmond neighborhoods.

As residential Richmond gradually moved toward the western boundary of the city, the owners of vacant lots that only a few years before could hardly be given away now found the same lots commanding high prices. It appeared that if Richmond continued to prosper and grow, the broad fields that swept westward from the city limits on either side of the Westham Road would also greatly appreciate in value. Acting on these speculations, a few local capitalists became interested in these lands not only for investment, but also as potential sites for their own suburban homes. This land, however, was still held in tracts of mostly one hundred acres as first established by Byrd's lottery and the approach to subdividing these large tracts as well as the prices to be paid became matters of lively local interest.

The Reverend John Buchanan

The most-coveted tract for investors was composed of several hundred acres, lying between the city limits and the Hermitage estate. This tract was owned by the esteemed Episcopal cleric John Buchanan (fig. 9).[12] The Reverend Buchanan, a native of Scotland, had inherited the property in 1787 from his oldest brother and benefactor, James,[13] and for years the good parson discouraged interested purchasers by explaining that the fraternal association gave the tract an indeterminate "pretium affectionis."[14] Buchanan stubbornly stuck by this position until as late as 1810 when escalating prices for suburban land, and possibly his own financial needs, induced him finally to part with most of the inheritance. He did, however, retain ownership of a farm that lay to the north of the Richmond Turnpike, called Buchanan's Spring. There a cool and clear-running spring,[15] set amid a grove of large trees, served as the gathering place of the Quoits Club, an illustrious group of Richmond citizens who met on genial Saturdays to eat, drink, and otherwise make merry.[16]

Bellville and Columbia

Among the early purchasers from Buchanan were two Petersburg merchants and brothers-in-law, John Bell and Philip Haxall, whose parcels familially adjoined one another.[17] Between 1810 and 1812, John Bell erected the elegant Bellville house[18] on his thirty-six-acre tract that stretched south from the Richmond Turnpike to the old Westham Road. Within a few years Haxall had completed his brick residence, later named Columbia, on fifteen acres located immediately to the west.

John Bell (fig. 10), another native of Scotland, had prospered as a commission merchant in Petersburg and apparently went to Richmond to establish a branch office and warehouse there.[19] Bell was obvi-

Fig. 9 The Reverend John Buchanan (1743–1822)

ously a man of refined sensibilities and he must have raised local eyebrows by importing a New England master builder, Alexander Parris, to plan and superintend the construction of his mansion.[20] While in Richmond, Parris was engaged to plan a house for attorney John Wickham that now serves as a portion of the Valentine Museum on Clay Street, and also the new governor's mansion in Capitol Square. All three of these Parris buildings were erected about 1810–1812 and therefore it would seem likely that Bellville was of the same general architectural format as the other two structures. To date no drawing has been located showing what the much-admired Bellville looked like.[21]

Soon after completing the house, Bell met unexpected financial reverses—some said this was because he had lavished too much time and money on what became known in some quarters as "Bell's Folly." An inventory attached to one of his creditor's deeds reveals the opulence of Bellville's furnishings: mahogany tables, chairs, beds and wardrobes, fine china, crystal, linens and silver, a "Piano Forte Musick" (valued at $250), two "Shakespear" prints, a painting of Saint John, and also twenty dozen bottles of Madeira wine along with sixty gallons of "old rum."[22] As Bell's financial difficulties deepened, his friends and relatives lent him a hand. In 1814 Bellville was conveniently "sold" to William Haxall, Philip Haxall's brother and business partner. The new owners allowed the Bells to stay on in residence until Haxall could find a buyer for the house and nearly twenty acres in December 1816.[23] The Bells then rented a new brick dwelling in Coutt's Addition. Bell was never able to recover financially and he was reported as being insolvent at the time of his death about 1832.[24]

John Bell's brother-in-law, Philip Haxall (fig. 11), had left Suffolk, England, in 1786 at the age of sixteen and with his two older brothers established a mercantile business in Petersburg. In 1809 Haxall relocated to Richmond to manage the Columbian Mills that he and his brother William had purchased from David Ross in 1809.[25] The river-powered mill was located at the foot of Twelfth Street and its production of flour would provide the Haxall family with handsome profits for several generations. Haxall apparently had bought his fifteen acres from Buchanan in 1810 with the intention of immediately subdividing them into lots for residential development. Coincident with his purchase he had prepared a plat showing sixteen lots arranged eight abreast between the Richmond Turnpike and the Westham Road, and the lots were called Haxall's Addition (fig. 13). Haxall was able to sell most of the lots but no houses were built until early in the following century. The sixty-foot street separating the lots was later named Lombardy Street.[26]

Undaunted by his brother-in-law's forced disposition of adjoining Bellville, Philip Haxall had com-

Fig. 10a John Bell (1770–1820) brought Alexander Parris to Richmond to plan and construct the fabled Bellville mansion.

Fig. 10b Mary Ann Walker Bell (1784–1847), wife of John Bell

pleted his dwelling, Columbia (fig. 14), by 1818. An early insurance policy shows the house as being forty-three by forty-five feet with a slate roof and also depicts a large kitchen and stable. The architectural style of the house—a flat and relatively tall and solid facade enlivened by rectangular panels recessed between the first- and second-story windows, elliptical fanlight over the entrance door, and low hipped roof crowned with a balustrade—are evocative of the Adamesque features employed by Alexander Parris in the governor's mansion, the Wickham House, and quite possibly at nearby Bellville. The residence, named after Haxall's downtown mill, still stands in somewhat altered form at the northeast corner of Grace and Lombardy Streets. Columbia's landscaped grounds were known especially for their beauty. Chief Justice and Mrs. John Marshall often drove out from town to enjoy the suburban air. The house was large enough to accommodate the Haxalls' eleven children and remained Philip Haxall's home until his death in 1831.[27]

The Reverend Buchanan's largest single property sale from his tract consisted of more than one hundred fifty acres lying on both sides of the Richmond Turnpike. The sale was made to another merchant with Scottish roots, John Graham, who also had investments in the coal business.[28] During the next few years, Graham would find purchasers for a few smaller lots from this parcel,[29] only one of which had been built on. By 1817, Mansfield Watkins, a resident of Manchester who operated a downtown Richmond wholesale grocery business, had erected a substantial brick house measuring forty by fifty feet on a four-acre tract fronting the Westham Road just east of the Bellville line.[30] Like John Bell, Watkins decorated his new residence with his own piano "fortie" and handsome mahogany furniture, as well as potted sweet orange, citron, lemon, and nutmeg trees.[31] Richmond printer Peter Cottom lived there from 1830 to 1847, and in 1852 the property became the home of John C. Shafer.[32]

Thomas Rutherfoord

The purchaser of most of the residue of John Graham's tract was Richmond businessman Thomas Rutherfoord (fig. 12), who at the time was making large investments in local real estate. The story of Thomas Rutherfoord is well known to many Richmonders; his often-cited *Autobiography* describes how he was dispatched to Richmond in 1784 at the age of eighteen to establish a branch for a Glasgow mercantile firm partially owned by his brother, his marriage into the established Winston family, and his financial success first as a tobacco trader and broker, then as a mill owner and a speculator in real estate. In 1793, feeling that "the lower part of the city is very unhealthy for children,"[33] Rutherfoord, after unsuccessfully negotiating for the Reverend Buchanan's tract, bought another hundred-

Fig. 11 Philip Haxall (1770–1831)

Fig. 12 Thomas Rutherfoord (1766–1852)

acre lot bordering the western limits of town from Buchanan's brother, Alexander. There he soon built a large and impressive residence.[34] Within a few years, Rutherfoord subdivided the surplus of this lot and other land to the north into a small but prestigious neighborhood called "Rutherfoord's Addition" that today includes the Commonwealth Club Historic District in the 400 block of West Franklin Street.

Rutherfoord kept this experience in mind. When affairs began to deteriorate between his adopted country and Great Britain following the Embargo of 1807, Rutherfoord, fearing that his large sums of paper money would become "expurged and reduced to nothing," turned to investment real estate as a hedge against the expected depreciation. During the summer months of 1814, Rutherfoord paid large sums of cash for the acquisition of some of the vacant lots that Philip Haxall had laid off from Columbia: an eleven-acre tract from the Bellville estate fronting along the north side of the Westham Road and more than fifty acres from John Graham of which thirty-five acres stretched from the town limits out to Bellville and Mansfield Watkins's lines south of the Richmond Turnpike.[35]

Meanwhile, John Mayo's fortunes had continued to prosper, and possibly finding the Hermitage a bit too rural or too modest for his elevated station in life, Mayo bought Bellville with its remaining acreage from William Haxall in 1816.[36] Mayo's oldest daughter, Maria, the first popularly recognized belle of Richmond's society, was being courted by the dashing General Winfield Scott, a hero of the War of 1812, and perhaps the Mayos felt their move to this elegant home would add materially to Maria's obvious physical charms. And so it proved. The nuptials were celebrated at Bellville on 11 March 1817—a memorable Richmond social event—with the Reverend Buchanan performing the ceremony. Unfortunately, Mayo was not able to enjoy the beauty of Bellville; he died in May 1818 at age fifty-eight, his obituary aptly calling him "a man of bold and enterprising nature."[37] His wife, Abigail Mayo, continued to live on at Bellville until it burned in 1841. Surprisingly, the Mayos' long-deserted home, the Hermitage, survived Bellville, not succumbing to fire until 1857. Nevertheless, it had been in a melancholy and neglected condition for years prior to its demise.[38]

A short time before his death, Mayo had subdivided his Hermitage lands lying south of the Richmond Turnpike into twenty-three multi-acre lots that he publicly offered for sale (fig. 15). Only a few years before, this venture would have been considered foolhardy even for the persistent Mayo, but by 1817 a period of feverish land speculation was evident in Richmond and most of Mayo's lots found eager buyers. Vacant land in and about the city proved to be far too scarce during these heady years that became known as the "flush times."

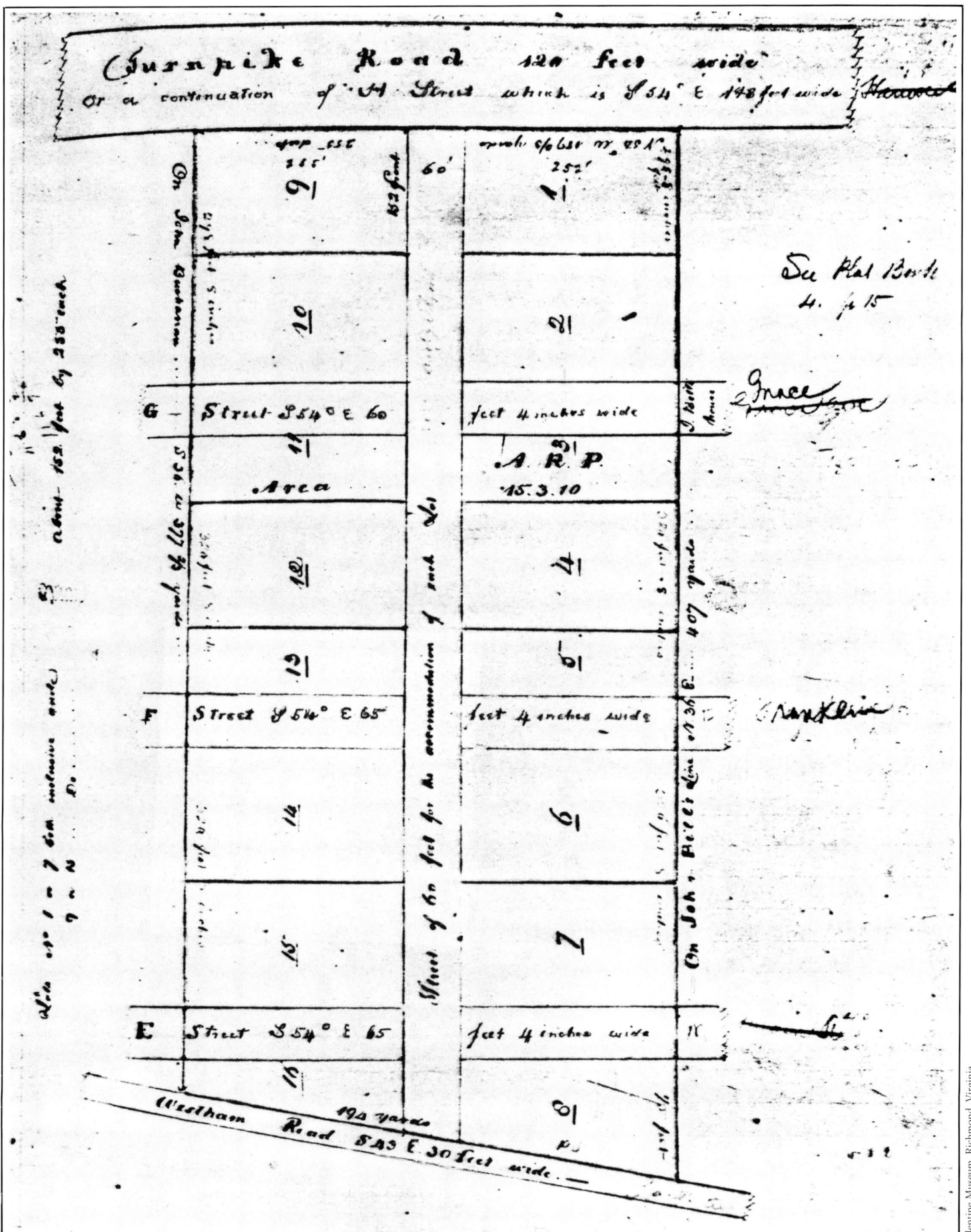

Fig. 13 "Haxall's Addition," a subdivision of sixteen lots on either side of the present Lombardy Street between Park Avenue (the Westham Road) and Broad Street (the Richmond Turnpike), was laid out by Philip Haxall in 1810. (Henrico County Plat Book)

Fig. 14 Columbia, built for Philip Haxall ca.1818, was later part of Richmond College.

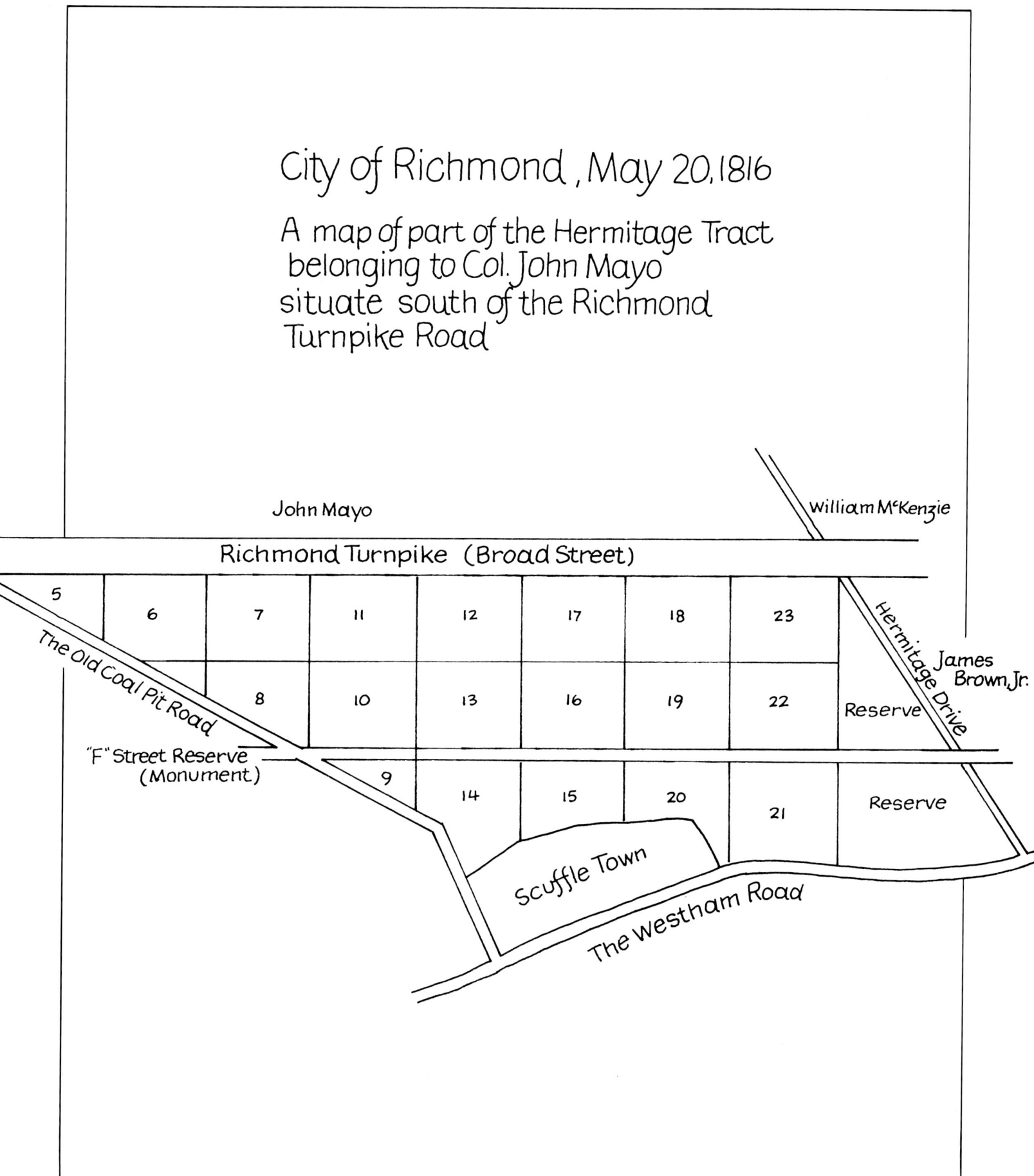

Fig. 15 Colonel John Mayo Jr. subdivided the southern portion of his Hermitage tract from the Richmond Turnpike (Broad Street) to the Westham Road (Park Avenue) about 1818 (redrawn from Henrico County Plat Book).

CHAPTER FOUR

The Flush Times

1817–1822

The conclusion of hostilities with Great Britain in 1815 did not dispel the then-widely accepted premise that real estate would continue to be a most desirable and profitable investment. In fact, the relaxation of bank-lending and repayment terms following the war made credit available to a wide segment of the population. This easy credit fueled an incredible amount of speculation in the purchase and sale of lots, squares, and larger parcels of undeveloped land in Richmond, as well as across the nation. These few years of furious buying and selling were later aptly called the "flush times" by Richmond writer Samuel Mordecai. He wrote about them with characteristic insight and wit:

> The limits of Richmond were too contracted for the imaginary population which was soon to overflow the city, and new towns or extensions of the old were tacked on in every direction. Corn-fields, Slashes and Piney thickets were laid out into streets and squares.... City lots proper advanced in price, two, three, five, aye, ten fold, and those in the suburban towns, displayed on a highly coloured plot,—but not so highly coloured as the description of those who plotted to catch purchasers,—instead of being sold by the acre at ten to fifty dollars, were retailed by the foot at ten to fifty times their former value.[1]

Landowners rushed to plat their land so that they could share in the profits; red flags waved and fluttered in the cornfields to show the eager speculators where these valuable investments were to be found; and by 1817 three men had embarked on the most ambitious Richmond real estate project since the Byrd lottery scheme. It was called the town of Sydney.[2]

The Town of Sydney

The town of Sydney was to be developed on part of the acreage accumulated by Colonel John Harvie Jr. (fig. 16), a native of Albemarle County and a close friend of Thomas Jefferson. Harvie had arrived in Richmond in 1781 to assume his government job as the register of the Virginia Land Office, which he held until 1791. Active militarily and politically in the Revolution, Harvie, a lawyer, had served as a member of the Continental Congress and was later a signer of the Articles of Confederation.[3] He immediately became involved in the governance of his adopted city. In 1782 he was appointed to the city council, three years later he was elected Richmond's fourth mayor, and in 1793 and 1794 he represented the city in the Virginia House of Delegates.

Fig. 16 Colonel John Harvie Jr. (1747–1807)

Valentine Museum, Richmond, Virginia

Chapter Four

In his role as register, Harvie became accustomed to dealing with vast tracts of land in the western territories,[4] and he soon turned his attention to real estate speculations about Richmond. In 1794, Harvie purchased eight of the hundred-acre Byrd lots, extending from the Westham Road south to the James River, that originally had been won in the lottery drawing by Scottish merchant James McCaul. Several months later, Harvie bought the remainder of Charles Price's four-hundred-acre tract adjoining Scuffletown, thereby giving himself twelve-hundred contiguous acres located just to the west of the city line.[5] By 1800, Harvie had also purchased the Belvidere estate from George Washington's nephew, Bushrod Washington.[6] Harvie still held his accumulated acreage when he died in 1807 at Belvidere. A secluded and wooded dell several hundred yards to the west of Belvidere was selected for his burial site. Forty years later this area would be laid out as the grounds of Hollywood Cemetery (fig. 17).

After Harvie's death his son Jaquelin Burwell Harvie managed the property.[7] Born in 1788, Jaquelin B. Harvie had served a brief stint as a midshipman in the United States Navy and then returned to Richmond after his father's demise to oversee the family estate. In 1813 he married Mary Marshall, the only daughter of the chief justice. During the flush times in Richmond, Harvie found himself in a most propitious situation as his father's holdings encompassed twelve hundred undeveloped acres in the near west end of Richmond including most of what would later become Richmond's Fan District. It would have seemed almost a malfeasance on his part if he had not taken advantage of this excellent opportunity. Yet Harvie was obviously a man of some prudence and the thought of tackling this large venture alone may have daunted him since he allowed two Richmond businessmen, Benjamin James Harris and George Winston, to participate with him in the development of his family's large holdings. Both Harris and Winston seemed eminently qualified for this enterprise.

Benjamin James Harris, a prosperous tobacco manufacturer with a large factory at the corner of Fourteenth and Franklin Streets, had also established a cotton mill located on the James River Canal. In 1808, Harris had purchased part of Council Chamber Hill where he erected the splendid mansion, Clifton, and in 1814 he bought the Belvidere house and its surrounding acreage from Colonel Harvie's estate.[8] Simultaneously with his venture with Harvie and Winston, Harris also developed thirty-five acres of the Belvidere tract lying south of Spring Street between Belvidere and Cherry Streets into seventy residential lots that he named Belvidera (fig. 18).[9]

George Winston was probably the best-known builder of the time in Richmond. He oversaw a number of apprentices who were bound to him or whose time he had bought. In addition to a lumberyard on Main Street, he operated a brickyard in Shed Town, in Richmond's East End, where he fired bricks to meet his own needs and to supply such projects as the erection of the State Penitentiary.[10] With an excellent reputation, he undertook the construction of many fine dwellings first on Church Hill and later farther west, including Thomas Rutherfoord's impressive 1795 mansion at Adams and Franklin Streets.[11] It was most likely Winston who, about 1817, built what may have been the first dwelling in the town of Sydney, a modest brick structure at 610 West Cary Street (moved in 1995 across the street to 617) now known as the Jacob House.

It would seem, then, based on the estates, reputations, and talents of these men, that the success of their venture was assured, especially during "flush times." By articles of agreement dated 10 August 1815,[12] Harvie promised to sell to Harris and Winston one-half of the land he had inherited from his father, which moiety was to be equal in value "in respect to quantity, quality, situation and every other circumstance" to the half Harvie would retain. Harris would receive three-quarters and Winston one-quarter, respectively, of their portion and each in turn agreed to pay Harvie $450 per acre, typically for flush times in five annual installments. As Harvie's inheritance had not yet actually been determined and segregated from the rest of his father's landed estate, the Virginia Superior Court of Chancery appointed William Brockenbrough, Thomas Taylor, and Robert Gamble as commissioners to partition the colonel's real estate between Jaquelin and the representatives of his deceased brother, Edwin James Harvie, who had died of injuries sustained in the 1811 Richmond Theatre fire. The commissioners promptly allocated to Jaquelin Harvie about five hundred and forty acres, almost all of which lay north of present-day Cary Street, then called the Westham Plank Road.[13] Thereafter, Harvie, Harris, and Winston "for the mutual advantage of all parties" laid off this land "in a town which they have called the Town of Sydney and have divided the same into squares and lots numbered from 1 to 536 and streets designated by particular names and for greater certainty caused a fair and accurate platt to be prepared of the Town of Sydney" (figs. 19a–b).[14]

Overleaf: Fig. 17 View of downtown Richmond from the future site of Hollywood Cemetery, near Belvidere, taken from Herman Böye's Map of Virginia, 1825

Chapter Four

Fig. 18 "Belvidera" subdivision map. In 1817 Benjamin J. Harris laid off most of the Belvidere estate into building lots that now make up the southern portion of the Oregon Hill neighborhood (redrawn from Henrico County Plat Book).

Most of the squares contained four lots of one acre each; Winston received about seventy while Harris was assigned more than two hundred. The east-west streets, which were named in alphabetical order from south to north, were to be sixty-six feet wide, the north-south streets fifty-two feet, and the alleys twenty feet.[15] The plat reveals that Sydney incorporated all of today's Fan District lying south of Park Avenue from Belvidere Street out to and beyond the Boulevard.

This 1817 plat is remarkable in that it appears almost identical to the present layout of the Fan District, although many of these streets would not actually appear until scores of years had passed. The street pattern of eastern Sydney formed a continuation of Harris's Belvidera plan to the south, but west of Morris Street the founders doglegged the east-west streets to run parallel with the Westham Plank Road, which formed the southern property line of Sydney.[16] In designing the town, the planners could not neatly drop a grid street-pattern into a square area; they had to confront the problem of how to place their new streets as they met the winding Westham Road, which divided the town of Sydney from Scuffletown and the other properties to the north.[17] They elected to bring their new streets straight into the Westham Road and there abruptly terminate them. This design resulted in the branching or fanning out of the new streets from the path of the Westham Road, which, when implemented, would create interesting and unexpected vistas as one proceeded out the old road from town. This placement also severed a number of small, irregularly shaped parcels that would prove impracticable to develop as building lots but that would later be admirably suitable for small neighborhood parks.

With the plat of the town of Sydney finished, Harvie, Harris, and Winston began to market their lots. At first they found a receptive public and a number of squares were sold on credit for the handsome price of more than a thousand dollars per acre. The deeds acknowledged that many of the streets were not yet in place but promised they would be built at "such time as public convenience shall require the opening." In the meantime, the purchasers were allowed to enclose the street area. For some reason Hanover Street was selected to be opened immediately and kept open "forever," but this did not actually occur until well after the Civil War.

This incredible land boom was totally dependent on the availability of easy credit, but by 1818 easy credit had begun to dry up. After defalcations by the Bank of the United States and reverses caused by a faltering economy, national and local banking regulations were again tightened, and bankers and sellers began looking for payments when due. Lenient extensions became a thing of the past. With neither credit nor cash available to repay or refinance obligations, borrowers had no choice but to ask their creditors to look to their mortgaged properties for repayment, and vast amounts of local real estate were thrown back on the market almost overnight. By 1819 grim foreclosure sales had replaced the gay real estate auctions in Richmond and across the nation. Mordecai vividly described this sudden transformation:

> Presto! change! The city and suburb lots were again on the market, but the prospects had changed as much as had the aspect of the cornfields; from waving blades and ears tipped with silken tassels, to dry stalks and refuse shucks. Sales were advertised, but where was the demand that was to double the cost? Alas! all were sellers and the only buyers were the original owners, who repurchased at half-price, or less, and never got the other half.[18]

Owners of land lying to the north of the Westham Road such as John Mayo Jr., Philip Haxall, and Thomas Rutherfoord were able to avoid acute financial distress primarily because they had other resources that allowed them to ride out the hard times, but both Mayo and Rutherfoord had still to take back properties they had sold at high flush-times prices and that were now practically worthless.[19] Mansfield Watkins was less fortunate and followed John Bell to financial ruin—in 1821 Watkins was thrown into the Henrico County jail on account of four outstanding judgment executions, and he was released only on his declaration of insolvency.[20]

The panic also devastated Harvie, Harris, and Winston. George Winston became the first casualty; his outstanding construction contracts in which he had invested his own capital were not honored, and he was arrested in the summer of 1820 for not paying his own obligations. His oath of insolvency did not deter his former partner Harris, who had bought Winston's note from Harvie, from directing that Winston's Sydney lots be sold at foreclosure. In 1821 many were auctioned. Philip Haxall, of nearby Columbia, bought eight one-acre lots at the distressed price of sixteen dollars each. Winston tried to salvage what he could by conveying property to his family, but these transfers were later set aside as being fraudulent.[21] George Winston found himself wiped out.

Benjamin James Harris soon followed. Scrambling madly to raise capital to offset his highly leveraged position, he found his real estate holdings were not worth nearly what he had paid for them just a few short years before. Harris traded back to Harvie at fifty dollars per acre some Sydney lots that he had agreed to buy from Harvie for four hundred and fifty dollars an acre. Within a year all of his assets including furniture, slaves, stock, and real estate were turned over to trustees for liquidation, but he was allowed "the necessary means of temporary support until he could get into a way of earning a livelihood for himself and his family."[22] Soon his trustees were advertising and selling all of his property including his Sydney lots, Belvidere, and even his tobacco business at rock-bottom prices. Harris was not to find prosperity again and he died insolvent in 1834.

Even Jaquelin Harvie did not escape unscathed. Anticipating the fat profits he would reap in the flush times (he actually did receive the 1816 payment from Harris and Winston), Harvie in 1817 built an imposing mansion at 916 East Clay Street. He also became involved in the Richmond Dock Company, the Belle Isle Rolling and Slitting Mill and Nail Manufactory, and the firm of Brockenbrough and Harvie, which operated a general store on Main Street offering "wainscoting, carpeting, swansdown, flannels and hosiery." Unlike Winston's and Harris's, Harvie's financial situation did not require an immediate liquidation of his Sydney holdings. But while Harvie would become a leader in Richmond's social, business, and civic life,[23] he never could rid himself entirely of debt. For twenty-five years he used his Sydney properties as collateral to secure his creditors. Harvie lived on until 1856 and was buried in the family plot at Hollywood Cemetery near his father—his obituary calling him "a gentleman of great energy and boldness of character as well as kindness of heart."[24]

Needless to say, the town of Sydney, once so ambitious and full of promise, ended up a faded dream that brought financial ruin to two of its founders and embarrassment to its third. Yet unlike Scuffletown, the town of Sydney left an indelible mark on the neighborhood. Because Harvie, Harris, and Winston had agreed that the streets of Sydney shown on their plat were dedicated for public use and would be opened when "necessary for the commerce of its inhabitants," subsequent property owners could not disregard the town plan even though most of the streets existed only on paper. This action taken in 1817 sealed the area's future street patterns, and thus influenced the character of the neighborhood that developed many years later.

Fig. 19a A view of development in the future Fan District Area in 1817. (Map of the City of Richmond by Richard Young, 1817)

Chapter Four

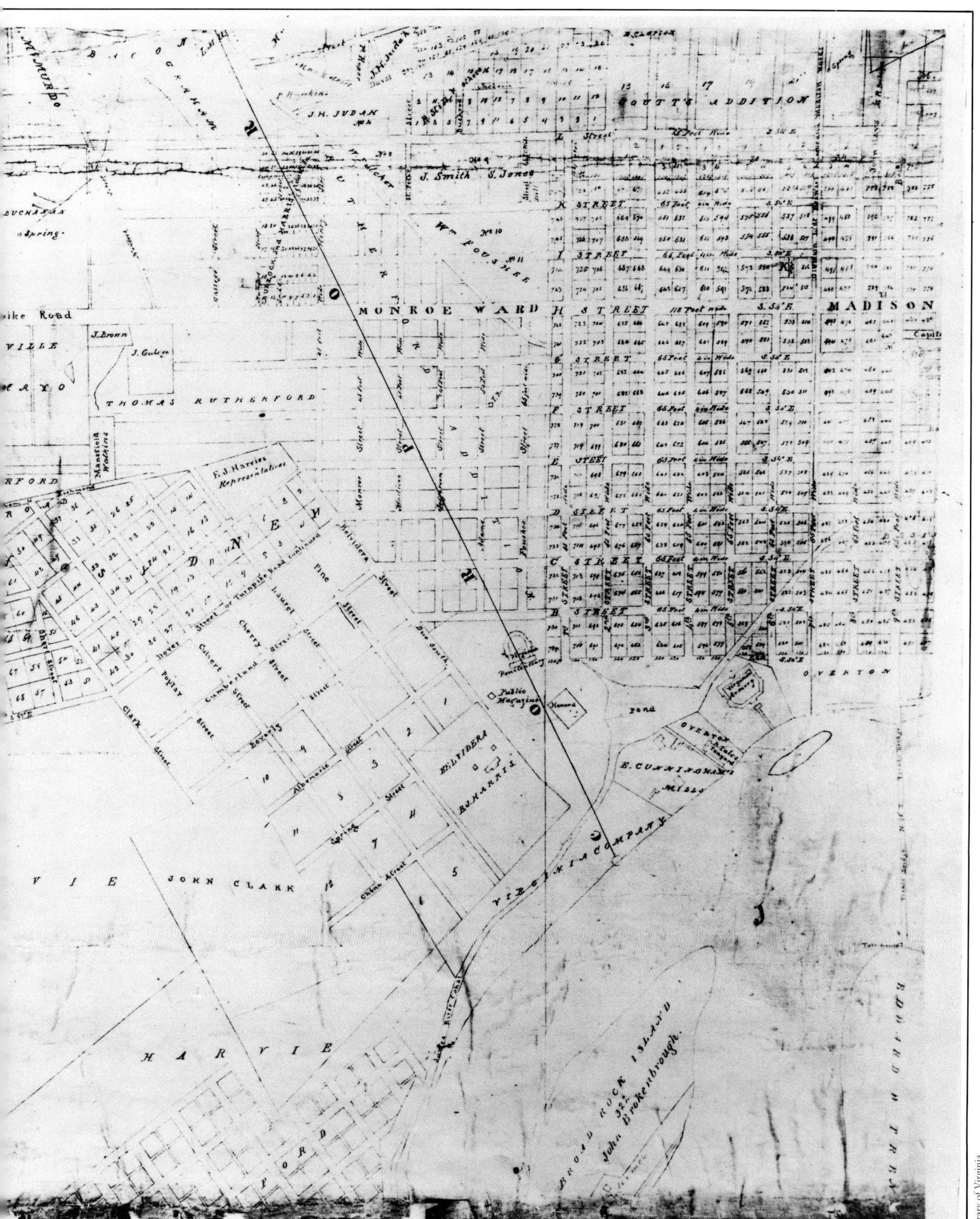

Chapter Four 38

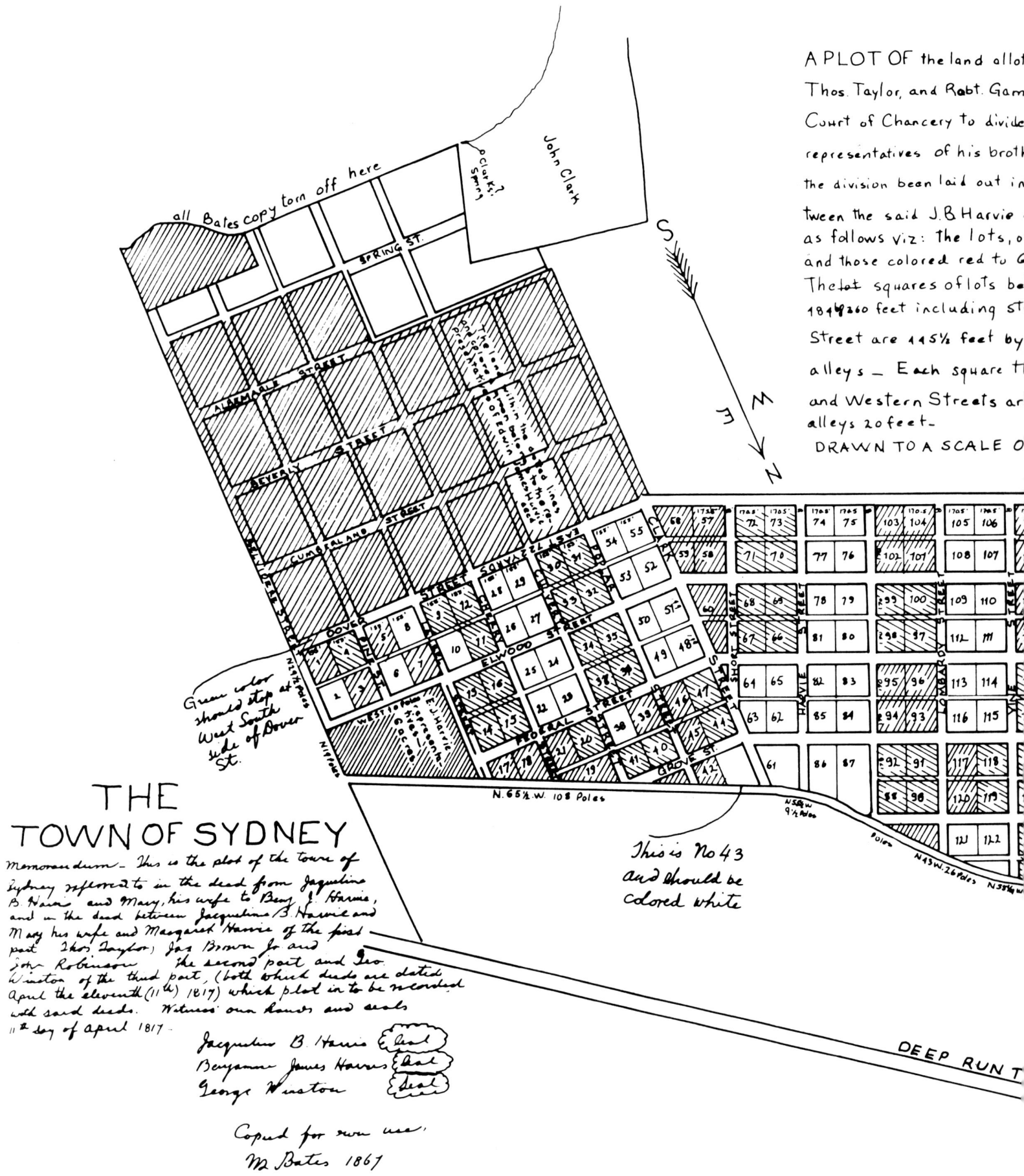

Fig. 19b A plat of the Town of Sydney envisioned by Jaquelin B. Harvie, George Winston, and Benjamin J. Harris during the "flush times." (Department of Public Works, City of Richmond)

Chapter Four

B. Harvie by William Brockenbrough
missoners appointed by the Supreme
d between said Harvie decd and the
in Jones Harvie decd which has since
streets and alleys and then, divided
Harris and George ~~Harris~~ Winston
colored yellow belong to J.B. Harvie
Winston and the white to B.J. Harris
Belvidere and Clark Streets are
d alleys — and all westward of Clark
t 3 inches including streets and
off contains 4 acres. The Eastern
t wide. The cross streets 50 feet and the

POLES TO AN INCH

Note: This is a copy of originals made by M Bates which map was in itself a copy, the original being on file in the Henrico County Court. The colorings of the lots hereon were taken from a copy marked by J T Redd present County Surveyor of Henrico County. Owing to the worn condition of Mr. Bate's copy it could not be traced and this map is plotted from the notes on Mr. Bate's.

<u>Therefore this map should not be used for buying and selling lots</u> but reference should be had to the maps and deeds on file in Court House Office.

Made for use in Hustings Office by CTO ___ ?___ for

January 7th 1887

CHAPTER FIVE

An Age of Contraction and Fear

1819–1835

The financial debacle of 1819 ushered in several decades of disappointing growth in Richmond. Business activity was crippled and many proprietors closed their doors and moved away. Between 1817 and 1820 the city experienced its first population decline since its founding with a loss of almost 16 percent of its people.[1] Economic and spiritual stagnation stubbornly held sway in Richmond until the mid-1830s—a span of years characterized by Mary Wingfield Scott as an "age of contraction and fear" during which progress and prosperity were almost imperceptible. The construction of well-appointed country seats seemed something from a long-distant past. Those city dwellers who had any money erected what they could afford on smaller lots in town, and until these lots were taken the market for suburban property remained uninspired.

Development about the Sydney neighborhood was further dampened by the fact that this land still lay entirely in Henrico County. The county fathers had no interest in allocating revenues derived from a rural tax base to build streets and other urban improvements for this area that they suspected would then be annexed into the city. After the completion of Columbia in 1818, only one residence of note, William Anderson's Warsaw, was built in the Sydney area over the next twenty years,[2] and the Belvidere and Hermitage houses began their long slides into oblivion. During this period, the normal developmental process of large tracts of land being broken down into smaller parcels to satiate buyer demand was reversed; now smaller properties were bought up at bargain prices and reassembled into large tracts by a few speculators who then patiently awaited the return of flush times. The few bidders who appeared at the many foreclosure sales of George Winston's and Benjamin J. Harris's former properties must have been rather incredulous when this land was promoted as numbered one-acre lots fronting on nonexistent streets. The lots in the more western areas of Sydney were offered in contiguous multi-acre groupings, and there was little haggling over the modest bids that were received and accepted for these properties.

One who moved to take advantage of these low prices was a twenty-seven-year-old Church Hill bricklayer, Richard Reins (fig. 20),[3] who would become a notable presence in an area that otherwise had very little identity of its own. In May 1825, Reins bid on thirty-five of Benjamin J. Harris's former lots, and a few months later bought the Scuffletown tavern building for $546 including the one-acre home lot that held the graves of Elisha and Phoebe Williams. Even though most of the other Scuffletown houses had vanished and the Westham Road to the west of the tavern building had now been abandoned, Reins moved his family there. Over the next thirty years Reins assiduously bought, sold, and promoted other Sydney lots, making him the most active of a small band of Sydney speculators.[4]

While Reins continued to earn his livelihood in the construction and contracting fields, he never ventured to build houses on his Sydney properties. Instead he devoted them to the production of fruits and vegetables. It is possible that during his ownership he re-instituted the tavern building as a public inn—in 1838 he included as part of the building's inventory six featherbeds and furnishings, four low-post and two curtained bedsteads, one set of dining tables, and eighteen Windsor chairs.[5] Also, many years later Reins was recollected as the owner of the "Scuffletown-Road Inn."[6] Yet by 1840, when Reins considered leaving Richmond for a construction job near Lynchburg with the James River and Kanawha Canal Company, his advertisement of sale made no mention of an inn. Instead he described a "Dwelling House contain[ing] seven rooms, five of which have fireplaces, with kitchen, smoke and carriage house, barn and stable all in good condition." Reins promoted the forty-two acres then surrounding the house as "rich land capable of producing as much of anything as can be grown in this neighborhood on a like quantity of land."[7]

Despite the lean times in the Sydney area, Reins undoubtedly played a part in the decision to move the Virginia Baptist Seminary to the Columbia estate there. In 1826 he joined First Baptist Church, then located downtown at the corner of College and Broad Streets, and within several years he was appointed one of the three trustees of the Virginia Baptist Education Society. The society in 1832 had purchased a farm at the north end of Hermitage Road to be used for a seminary to train students for the ministry. This rather remote site proved unsatisfactory, however, and two years later Reins and the other trustees elected to move the seminary closer to town. They purchased the Columbia house from Philip Haxall's widow, along with the eight easternmost lots of the old Haxall's Addition and also David Walker's former five-acre garden plot.[8] In 1840, the seminary was reorganized and rechartered as the more secular Richmond Col-

Chapter Five

Fig. 20 Richard Reins (1796–1871)

Fig. 21 Anthony Robinson Jr. (1771–1851)

lege. Reins received an appointment to the first board of trustees. From its inception, the college provided stability and prestige to this area, and in time its spacious and well-tended grounds would attract new institutional and residential development to the neighborhood. Reins continued to be a presence about Sydney until his death in 1871.

Another man who accumulated lots in the western end of Sydney was Anthony Robinson Jr. (fig. 21). Like Richard Reins, Robinson[9] began bidding on large numbers of contiguous lots located in western Sydney, and during the next twenty-six years he assembled more than one hundred and twenty acres. Robinson's holdings became known as the Grove. There he frequently retired from his house in town to raise crops and livestock in friendly competition with his brother John, who owned the adjoining farm to the south, Poplar Vale, which later became part of Byrd Park. Robinson Street in the town of Sydney appears to have been named after John rather than Anthony Robinson as Poplar Vale lay at the southern terminus of the street and in 1817 Anthony owned no property in the area, having returned to Richmond from Williamsburg only a few years before. While Anthony Robinson did build a cottage on his Grove property, the present Robinson House standing today in the parking area of the Virginia Museum of Fine Arts appears to have been built by his family after Robinson's death in 1851.[10] As both Reins and Robinson farmed their accumulated Sydney lots, those portions of the Westham and Coalpit Roads lying west of the tavern building soon disappeared under the plow, and the importance that these roads had played in Richmond's development became, like Scuffletown, only a memory.[11]

A third speculator in Sydney, William C. Allen, arrived in Richmond from King William County a few years before Richard Reins and like Reins he also entered into a bricklayer's apprenticeship. Allen would be much more successful in the building trade than Reins, however. While Richmond gradually moved toward prosperity during the 1830s, Allen received commissions for many residential and commercial jobs throughout the city, and he ventured into speculative construction on his own account as well.[12] As the pace of building quickened during the late 1830s and early 1840s, Allen served as both architect and contractor in this expansion, his obituary later noting "the growth of his fortune marked in many ways the improvement

Chapter Five

Fig. 22a Edgar Allan Poe (1809–1849) visited Susan Talley at Talavera.

Fig. 22b Susan Talley Weiss, Poe's youthful admirer

Fig. 22c Talavera, now 2315 West Grace Street, the home of the Talley family, was built in 1838.

of the city."[13] Allen erected a number of town-house rows within the city that he held as rental property. The income allowed him to retire to the handsome residence he built for himself in 1855 at the southeast corner of Sixth and Franklin Streets.

As Allen witnessed the renewed growth of the downtown area, he recognized the inevitability of the city's western expansion and thus as early as 1830 had begun to reassemble portions of John Buchanan's and John Mayo's former tracts lying west of Lombardy Street and north of the Westham Road. One result of his efforts was an impressive fifty-eight-acre tract that became popularly known as "the Allen Lot" and that still later would be laid off by his son Otway for the Lee statue and for Monument Avenue as well. During the late 1840s and the 1850s, Allen also bought in piecemeal fashion most of that part of Sydney located between Lombardy and Granby Streets. He made no attempt to develop these properties, probably recognizing that the time was not quite right. Thus it would be his children who would become the financial beneficiaries of his foresight.[14]

Just to the west of the Allen lot, Thomas Talley reassembled twenty-five acres from John Mayo Jr.'s abortive Hermitage subdivision and in 1838 erected a farmhouse on this land that he named Talavera. There Talley, a grocer, developed what was known as a "market garden" where he grew fruits and vegetables for sale at his downtown store. The house may still be found in the 2300 block of West Grace Street (fig. 22c), having survived primarily because of its association with Edgar Allan Poe (fig. 22a).[15] Even though Poe had not resided in Richmond since 1837, he did return periodically to visit friends and with his sister, Rosalie, who came to live with the McKenzie family in another house not far from Talavera.[16] At Talavera he became acquainted with Talley's daughter Susan (fig. 22b). When in the vicinity, Poe would call at Talavera to chat with the admiring young girl, and in a later memoir Susan Talley Weiss would write that on the last night Poe spent in Richmond before his fatal return to Baltimore, "a brilliant meteor appeared in the sky directly over his head, and vanished."[17]

Like their western counterparts, the lots in eastern Sydney not held by Jaquelin Harvie were also sold at public auction, but their proximity to town stimulated a bit more interest and resulted in a more numerous and diverse roster of owners. These lots traded hands with

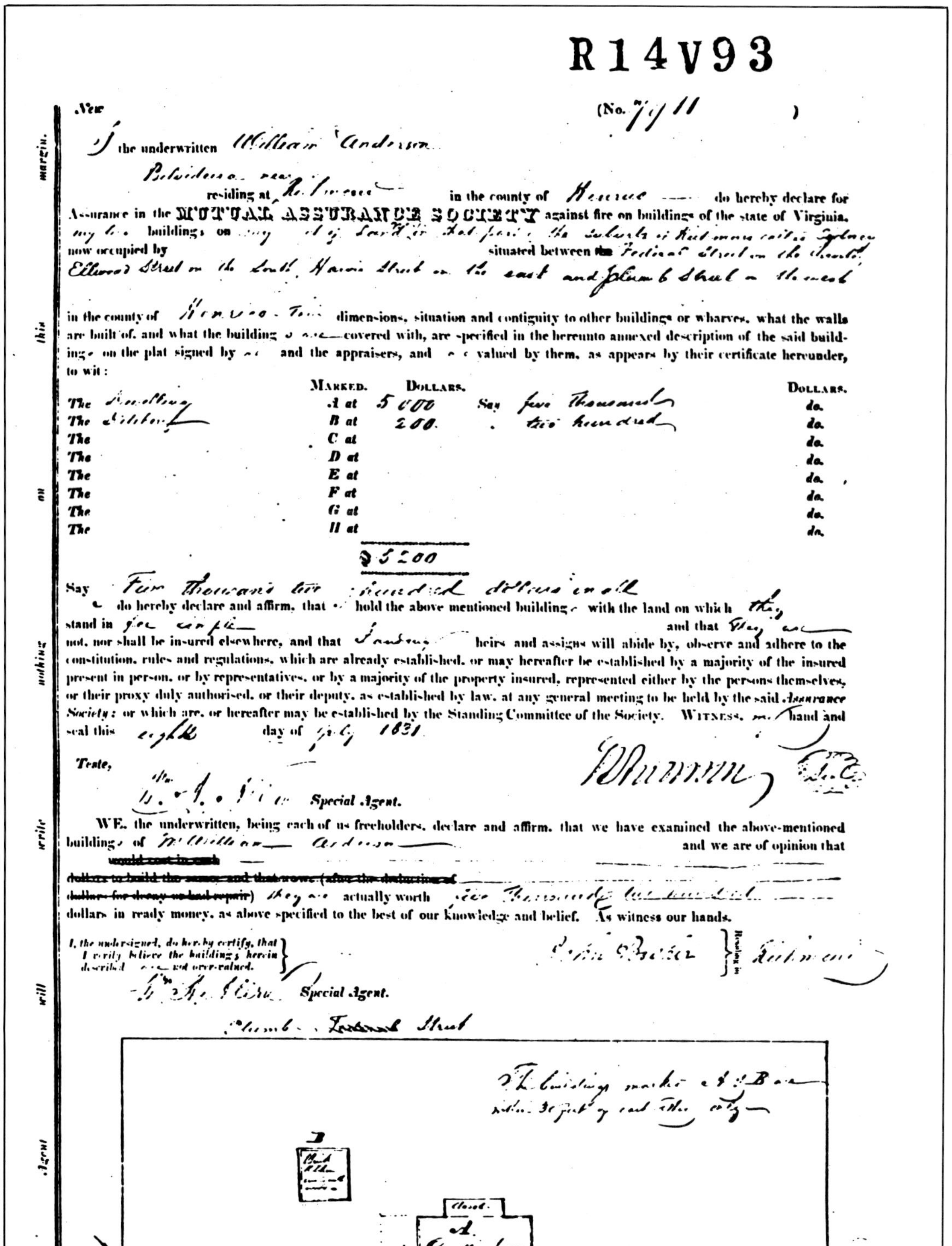

R14V93

New (No. 7711)

I the underwritten William Anderson
Belvidere near
residing at Richmond in the county of Henrico do hereby declare for
Assurance in the MUTUAL ASSURANCE SOCIETY against fire on buildings of the state of Virginia.
my two buildings on
now occupied by situated between the Federal Street on the north
Elwood Street on the south, Harris Street on the east and Plumb Street on the west
in the county of Henrico dimensions, situation and contiguity to other buildings or wharves, what the walls are built of, and what the building is covered with, are specified in the hereunto annexed description of the said buildings on the plat signed by and the appraisers, and valued by them, as appears by their certificate hereunder, to wit:

	Marked.	Dollars.		Dollars.
The Dwelling	A at	5000	Say five Thousand	do.
The Kitchen	B at	200.	two hundred	do.
The	C at			do.
The	D at			do.
The	E at			do.
The	F at			do.
The	G at			do.
The	H at			do.
		$5200		

Say Five thousand two hundred dollars in all
I do hereby declare and affirm, that I hold the above mentioned buildings with the land on which they stand in fee simple and that they are not, nor shall be insured elsewhere, and that I and my heirs and assigns will abide by, observe and adhere to the constitution, rules and regulations, which are already established, or may hereafter be established by a majority of the insured present in person, or by representatives, or by a majority of the property insured, represented either by the persons themselves, or their proxy duly authorised, or their deputy, as established by law, at any general meeting to be held by the said Assurance Society; or which are, or hereafter may be established by the Standing Committee of the Society. Witness, my hand and seal this eighth day of July 1831

Teste,
Special Agent.

W Anderson (Seal)

WE, the underwritten, being each of us freeholders, declare and affirm, that we have examined the above-mentioned buildings of Mr. William Anderson and we are of opinion that ~~would cost in cash~~
~~dollars to build the same, and that now (after the deduction of~~
~~dollars for decay or bad repair)~~ they are actually worth five Thousand two hundred
dollars in ready money, as above specified to the best of our knowledge and belief. As witness our hands.

I, the undersigned, do hereby certify, that I verily believe the buildings herein described are not over-valued.
Special Agent.

Residing in Richmond

Plumb Street

The buildings marked A & B are within 30 feet of each other only

A
Dwelling house

Elwood Street

Federal Street

Fig. 23 Mutual Assurance Society policy insuring William Anderson's house, Warsaw, 8 July 1831

more frequency, and on 30 August 1830 another Richmond grocer, William Anderson, bought the Sydney square bounded by Floyd, Harvie, Main, and Plum Streets. There he shortly completed a commodious brick dwelling that he named Warsaw.[18] Warsaw would prove to be the only substantial new house built in the Sydney area during the period from 1819 to 1838.

The business career of William Anderson revealed that local occupations dealing in basic and necessary products could still turn a profit even during these years of economic drought. Revenues from his large grocery business located on Main Street between Fourteenth and Fifteenth Streets allowed Anderson to invest in other downtown properties. Insurance records indicate that he became the owner of such diverse businesses as lumberyards, a soap and candle factory, a barber shop, a hat and millinery store, and even the Washington Tavern located at the northwest corner of Ninth and Grace Streets.[19] In 1824 Anderson had also purchased the Belvidere house from Benjamin J. Harris's trustees, and he soon moved there from his home on Franklin Street. Within a few years, commercial and industrial development along the canal and riverbank, as well as the close proximity of the expanding State Penitentiary, made this area surrounding the old Byrd residence unfashionable and Anderson vacated Belvidere soon after Warsaw's completion.

Little is known about Warsaw's original appearance. Insurance records show it as a substantial forty-eight-by-twenty-two-foot structure of two stories fronting on Harvie Street. It had a thirty-by-thirty-foot one-story brick rear section, along which ran a portico on the southern exposure looking to the river (fig. 23).[20] Warsaw was distinguished by its spacious four-lot square. The house was situated on a knoll on the northeast corner of the property behind which lay a courtyard holding a stable, servants' quarters, and other appurtenant buildings. Anderson died soon after finishing Warsaw, but the house remained in the Anderson-Gilmer family for many years. During the late 1870s, it was purchased and then enveloped in a large structure built and operated as the Saint Sophia Home for Old People by the Little Sisters of the Poor.[21] After more than one hundred years of ministry at this location, the nuns moved on to a new facility in the 1970s and the old structure was converted into a handsome condominium project named the Warsaw.

During these years of material poverty, the Belvidere house and Mayo's Hermitage were neglected and fell into disrepair. Shortly after moving to Warsaw, Anderson attempted to sell Belvidere but found no buyers. He then converted the old residence to rental property and for the next twenty years it suffered abuse by uncaring tenants. With its rich historical patina so physically desecrated, Belvidere was no longer considered a local historical treasure. When it caught fire and burned to the ground in 1857 hardly any mention was made in the local press of the passing of this Richmond landmark.[22]

The fate of the Hermitage house is a bit more puzzling. It is possible that after the Mayos moved to Bellville in 1818, Colonel Mayo used the house and its immediate grounds as the quarters for his extensive labor force—a force he needed to keep his bridge in repair as well as to farm his hundreds of surrounding acres—and that Mrs. Mayo continued this use after her husband's death. Increasing commercial traffic on the nearby Richmond Turnpike and the new main line of the Richmond, Potomac & Fredericksburg Railroad, which had been laid by the railroad in 1835 and which passed not far from the house, may have also disrupted the solitude and serenity that was the principal charm of the Hermitage. In any event, by the mid-1840s the Hermitage stood vacant and abandoned. Poe's Mrs. Weiss recalled a visit made by the poet to the "Hermitage Wood" and to a house he had known as a boy:

> Entering the deserted house, he passed from room to room with a grave, abstracted look, and removed his hat, as if involuntarily, on entering the saloon, where in old times many a brilliant company had assembled. Seated in one of the deep windows, over which now grew masses of ivy, his memory must have bourne him back to former scenes. . . . The light of the setting sun shone through the drooping ivy-boughs into the ghostly room, and the tattered and mildewed paper-hangings, with their faded tracery of rose garlands, waved fitfully in the autumn breeze.[23]

The Hermitage lingered on in this dilapidated state until 1857, when it too was consumed by fire.

Despite the hard times and unhappy demise of well-known Sydney properties, the revitalization of the James River Canal and the age of railroading would soon create a resurgence of business activity in Richmond and with it an increased residential expansion to the west.

CHAPTER SIX

The Canal, Railroads, and Heightened Prospects

1836–1861

While most of the 1830s had been a time of little material progress for many of Richmond's citizens, the state's internal improvements program continued apace and a number of public works projects crucial to the future economic welfare of the city moved forward. Chartered in 1832 as a joint-stock company, the James River and Kanawha Canal Company took over the stalled efforts of the James River Company to connect Tidewater Virginia and the navigable waters of the Ohio Valley with a canal system. Richmonders rejoiced when it was announced that the necessary stock had been subscribed. Some even speculated that on the completion of the venture, the commercial transactions of the city would immediately increase five- to tenfold.[1] The day of the railroad was also fast approaching; on 13 February 1836 the first railroad train ever to leave Richmond started its twenty-mile trek along the new tracks of the Richmond, Fredericksburg & Potomac Railroad Company, and within the next several years the lines of the Richmond and Petersburg and the Richmond and Louisa Railroads were also opened.

Despite two minor economic downturns that occurred in 1834 and 1837, the promise of a city connected by water and rail to the major markets of the country broke the apathy that had held Richmond in its grip for several decades. And with these heightened prospects, new capital flowed into Richmond in anticipation of better times. The canal and the railroads offered wider markets for the city's established iron, tobacco, flour, textile, and paper trades, and these major industries in turn generated smaller businesses, providing increased employment and profits.

This wave of business activity peripherally affected Sydney. The Tredegar Iron Works and the other industries that sprang up along the canal and on Belle Isle, particularly those fabricating iron,[2] together with the expansion of the State Penitentiary, spawned satellite blue-collar housing on Oregon Hill and in Benjamin J. Harris's former Belvidera subdivision (fig. 24). Other blue-collar workers were drawn to settle there, and the neighborhood started to push up into Sydney along Cary and Main Streets. In 1843 Jaquelin Harvie began to unload his Sydney lots east of Cherry Street and four years later parted with almost all of the rest of his Sydney holdings.[3] A few small businesses

Fig. 24 Lithograph of Richmond in 1854 by William MacLeod. The industrialization along the river is evident.

Fig. 25 The Jacob house on its new site at 617 West Cary Street

Fig. 26 This house, built by Silas Beazley in the 900 block of West Main Street in the 1840s, was replaced by The Mosque, currently called Richmond's Landmark Theatre.

took root along the West Cary–Main Street corridors to provide services to this gradually expanding neighborhood and also to the industries located nearby.

The majority of these workers' cottages were plain, small, frame structures. Some of them are still extant in that section that has become known as Oregon Hill—the original Oregon Hill settlement was located to the east of Belvidere Street. The scattered residences that did appear along Cary and Main Streets in Sydney were of more substantial construction, possibly due to their location on these through streets that gave desirable access to the downtown. Yet their owners appeared to have had social or business connections in this neighborhood rather than in the city proper. All these antebellum houses but one have since been demolished. The Federal-style Jacob House, which stands at 617 West Cary Street (fig. 25), was built perhaps as early as 1817 by George Winston and then enlarged from two bays to three in 1838 by John Jacob Sr., who purchased the property in 1832. Jacob was an assistant superintendent of the Virginia State Penitentiary just a few blocks to the southeast.[4]

Another example of a solid middle-class house was built by Silas Beazley (fig. 26) on the future site of what was called the Mosque but as of this writing is known as Richmond's Landmark Theater. Beazley was a house builder with a shop at Main and Third Streets and his dwelling, while frame, reflected a modest influence of the Greek Revival style, then very much in vogue in the more-substantial brick houses being constructed farther downtown, especially around Fifth Street. The house faced Main Street at the corner of Laurel and was later occupied by Adolph Beutel, a tailor.

During the years between the sale of Jaquelin B. Harvie's lower Sydney lots and the Civil War, these portions of Main and Cary Streets and the cross streets were well built up with an assortment of structures whose residents exhibited a rich variety of occupations. The 1860 city directory lists a number of grocers and carpenters, a teamster who worked out of Shockoe Slip, a huckster, a well-digger, a horse trader, a watchman at the Gallego Mills, a printer, and John Strong who captained a packet boat. This vitality also spread as far as the lower part of Floyd Avenue: Frank W. Hagermeyer is listed as a dairyman living between Morris and Harrison Streets, along with blacksmith James H. Oliver and gardener Michael Lyons. Another Floyd Avenue resident was Edward Newman who sold flowers at the First Market downtown; Patrick Gall was a molder at William Hubard's nearby foundry.

In the area of eastern Sydney lying north of Floyd Avenue a few houses also appeared but in a less-concentrated and more-random pattern than those to the south. The occupants of these residences had closer

Fig. 27 Dr. Reuben Meredith built this house in 1839 at the northwest corner of Grove Avenue and Harvie Street (demolished).

ties with the world of downtown, and it appears that this area was somehow designated for future middle-class settlement even though at the time demand for this housing was light.[5] Selecting the block bounded by Park and Grove Avenues and Harvie and Plum Streets, in 1839 Dr. Reuben Meredith, of Cedar Grove, Hanover County, erected a large brick dwelling that almost rivaled Warsaw in assessed value (fig. 27). As shown in the photograph, the two-story house sat on a raised basement, fronting, as Warsaw did, on Harvie Street; yet given the chimney arrangement the entrance may have originally faced Grove Avenue. Meredith had eight children and their education was of paramount importance to him. Before he died in 1841 he had directed "if my wife does not wish to reside in my house in the Town of Sydney in the suburbs of the City of Richmond" then the house should be sold or rented and the proceeds used for the education of his children. By 1850, H. J. Christian was leasing the property from Meredith's executors for an annual rent of $125.[6] In 1881 the house was bought and used for the Baptist Home for Aged Women and then in 1912 it was replaced by the present structure standing at the northwest corner of Grove Avenue and Harvie Street.[7]

In 1840, on the block located between that of the Meredith house and Warsaw, Edward F. Peticolas (fig. 28) began constructing what soon became a wondrous neighborhood landmark. Peticolas was the son of French artist and émigré, Phillippe A. Peticolas, who was reported to have settled in Richmond in 1804 at the urgings of wealthy flour miller Joseph Gallego. Edward was raised in Richmond where his artistic abilities were soon recognized and then sent to Europe to study under several artists of note.[8] On his return to Richmond, he became a respected painter primarily of miniature portraits.[9] In midlife Peticolas's temperament became increasingly fragile, and possibly to escape the tensions of the city he sought a retreat in the quiet suburbs of Sydney where he devoted himself to the cultivation of roses, fruits, and grapes. Unfortunately he did not find peace there, his eccentricities being reflected in his house, which was dubbed "the Castle." Robert Alonzo Brock, later secretary of the Southern Historical Society, was duly impressed as a boy by this weird old man and his bizarre creation:

> The "castle" was of wood, chiefly; a heterogeneous mass in form and material defying literal description. There were many additions in different stages of completion, and turrets varied

Chapter Six

Fig. 28 Edward F. Peticolas (1793–ca. 1853). This drawing by William J. Hubard was apparently done at the urging of his friend and patron, Mann S. Valentine II. Valentine wrote on the drawing: "The old man first refused to have a sketch made of him and when he consented to having it done he wished to 'dress'—that is, change his picturesque garb for his best clothes. Hubard . . . pretended consent to his wishes."

Fig. 29 Self-portrait, William J. Hubard (1807–1862). Hubard, a gifted artist, cast statues and cannons and experimented with the manufacture of munitions at his Grove Avenue house and foundry. On 13 February 1862, Hubard was mortally injured by an accidental explosion.

Fig. 30a Samuel J. Rutherfoord (1806–1880), son of Thomas Rutherfoord

Fig. 30b Frances Watson Rutherfoord, wife of Samuel Rutherfoord

in dimensions and attitude; the whole unpainted, and some portions in a course of decay, whilst others were constantly receiving the addition of new boards or framing timbers.[10]

Within a few years Peticolas was formally adjudged a lunatic and his son Dr. Arthur Edward Peticolas subdivided and began to sell off the square, thus necessitating the dismantling of this rather wild pleasure dome of fancy.[11] The elder Peticolas died shortly thereafter.

Undeterred by Peticolas's disregard of neighborhood propriety, leather-and-lumber merchant James G. Watson built two brick houses several blocks down Grove Avenue from the Castle, one in 1840 and the other in 1841.[12] They were located on the north side of Grove between Harrison and Morris Streets. Watson probably lived in the easternmost house as it was the larger of the two, with basement, two stories, and garret along with the usual detached kitchen and stable, the latter exiting onto the Westham Road. It also seems likely that Watson built the other house for his daughter, Frances (fig. 30b), who had married Samuel J. Rutherfoord (fig. 30a), fifth son of Thomas Rutherfoord. After withdrawing from his father's business enterprises, Samuel Rutherfoord and his bride, as his father would write, "removed . . . to a house about half a mile west of my residence where Sam is principally employed in farming operations which he seems to take considerable delight in, and I think he would succeed in that line of business were he on a suitable farm with more favorable prospects than at present."[13] The younger Rutherfoord's farming operations were mostly conducted on his father's lands, which lay to the north of the Westham Road and to the west of Laurel Street. By 1843 Thomas Rutherfoord began to deed this land over to his son, thus assuring the latter's future career as a real estate developer. Within a few years Samuel Rutherfoord built his own house at the corner of Grace and Laurel Streets but moved back to the family's Franklin Street house after his father's death in 1852.[14]

By 1847 Captain Christopher Q. Tompkins had purchased James Watson's home place. After a credible military career, Tompkins had been attracted to Richmond by the many new iron businesses that were springing up along the canal. Probably inspired by the example of his West Point classmate, Joseph Reid Anderson—the master of the now-prosperous Tredegar Iron Works—Tompkins bought the Virginia Steel Company in 1848. Along with partner Walter Gwynn, Tompkins operated the business under the name of the Richmond Iron and Steel Works. While in residence on Grove Avenue, Tompkins purchased the triangular lot to the east of his house for $75 from Jaquelin Harvie and there he tended a garden. When Harrison Street was opened later, this garden would become the present park commemorating the Richmond Howitzers.[15]

Another iron manufacturer, Charles Y. Morriss, followed Tompkins as the next owner of this house. Soon after his 1854 purchase,[16] Morriss, probably to accommodate his growing family, built a two-story addition on the east side of the house looking to the garden.[17] He also bought a three-acre parcel immediately north across Park Avenue that later would hold the 1000 block of West Avenue.[18] Morriss apparently went to Richmond from Buckingham County to become co-owner with Joseph Anderson of the Tredegar Rolling Mill under the name of Anderson, Morriss and Company. Anderson then sold the majority interest in the mill to Morriss and to Anderson's head clerk, John F. Tanner, who under their joint names operated the mill for a little more than two years. When Anderson bought the mill back in 1859, Morriss constructed, on the eve of the Civil War, a large sugar refinery in Rocketts that he was able to sell in 1871 for $85,000. Morriss lived in the Sydney house until his death in 1884. Clarke Street was later renamed Morris (without the second *s*) to denote his long and stable tenure within the neighborhood.

James G. Watson's other brick house to the west of the Tompkins-Morriss residence became in 1848 the home of another established artist, William J. Hubard (fig. 29).[19] Born in England in 1807, Hubard had by the 1830s become a portrait painter of note along the eastern seaboard. Initially he used Gloucester County as his home base—he married into the well-connected Tabb family there—but moved to Richmond in search of a more receptive market for his work. His paintings of prominent Richmond subjects, many now owned by the Valentine Museum, attest to his popularity. His Sydney neighbor, Captain Tompkins, was an old Gloucester acquaintance.

Probably influenced by Tompkins, Hubard strayed from his painting career after moving to Sydney, and he too entered the foundry business. Hubard opted, however, to cast works of art rather than machine parts. He obtained the state legislature's permission to reproduce Houdon's famed statue of George Washington, which still stands in the State Capitol; and when Peticolas's nearby Castle square was divided into lots and sold due to his insanity, Hubard in 1853 bought two in the middle of the square where he built a brick foundry.[20] After many disappointments, Hubard finally managed to cast six "perfect" reproductions of the Washington statue. Many years later one of these statues would be placed for a time in Monroe Park to become Richmond's "Washington Monument."[21] The other five casts are presently found at such diverse places as the Virginia Military Institute, Lafayette Park in Saint Louis, Missouri, the State Capitol grounds in Raleigh, North Carolina, and in Columbia, South Carolina, and at the Metropolitan Museum of Art in New York City.

A few other brick houses were added to this little suburban enclave in eastern Sydney during the 1840s and 1850s including one constructed in 1847 by Lawson H. Dance directly across Harvie Street from Warsaw. Dance, probably the successful blacksmith with a shop and forge located on Main Street, invested in a number of Sydney lots around Warsaw and actually turned a profit on their resale. This house was rebuilt as a "beautiful villa" during the war years but little else has been found concerning its history.[22] In 1851 grocer Benjamin W. Totty erected two connected brick-tenements across Grove Avenue from the old Mansfield Watkins house. It seems probable that the house standing at 1003 Grove Avenue (fig. 31), although greatly altered, is the westernmost Totty tenement, the twin having been demolished when the present corner town house was constructed.[23] The widow Elizabeth Jennings built a brick house farther west about 1857 on the southeast corner of Harvie Street and Grove Avenue. The dwelling measured twenty-five by thirty-five feet and had a tin roof. Like Warsaw, a portico ran along its southern side offering a view toward the river as well as of the penitentiary.[24]

With its tax base expanding during this period of growth, the city drifted into the urban-parks movement that was finding expression in other municipal centers across the nation. In 1851, the Richmond City Council, citing the exigencies of "invigorating air" and the "interchange of social affections" for its citizenry, formed a committee to investigate whether public parks should be established on Church Hill, Gamble's Hill, and "at Samuel Rutherfoords Esq. and at Joseph Jacksons Esq."[25] The immediate goal of this early venture into city planning was of course to create a more beautiful and a healthier city; yet the council also anticipated that these public green spaces, tastefully established and laid out, would add to the city's tax base by attracting new residential development around each park. Dr. John P. Little, writing in 1851 in the *Southern Literary Messenger*, echoed these sentiments:

> This city needs other squares to be laid off for exercise and pleasure, beside the one already existing. The upper part, which is now rapidly increasing, especially requires this improvement; if the ground was now secured and planted with trees, it would soon be surrounded with handsome blocks of houses, and the adjoining lots be very much increased in value.[26]

The potential sites were each strategically located near one of the four edges of Richmond—east, south, west, and north—all of which at this time had room for growth.

Fig. 31 This house, at 1003 Grove Avenue, is probably the altered survivor of a pair of houses built in 1851 by Benjamin W. Totty.

The Richmond City Council soon selected the West End Rutherfoord site along with those on Church and Gamble's Hills.[27] The council promptly made arrangements to acquire several acres of Samuel Rutherfoord's patrimony as well as a large field filled with scrub and blackberry bushes, lying just to the south across the Westham Road.[28] This field had been omitted from the plan of the Town of Sydney, since the court had allocated it to the estate of Jaquelin Harvie's deceased brother Edwin during the partition of Colonel Harvie's properties. Thus it remained intact and unencumbered by real or paper streets. This new park area was first called Western Square, but by May 1855 it had been renamed Monroe Square as the grounds abutted the Monroe Ward of the city.[29]

Hardly had the land been acquired and the bisecting Westham Road closed and abandoned[30] than city council received a request from the Virginia State Agricultural Society to use one of the new public squares on 1 November 1853 for its first cattle show and agricultural fair. Even though the request had strings attached—the society asked that the grounds be fenced and public water be made available on the site—councilmen were aware of the benefits that would accrue to the city from such a statewide annual convention. They quickly directed the city engineer to draw up plans laying off the Western Square for these purposes (figs. 32a–c).[31] Because of his military background, Captain Christopher Q. Tompkins, who had not yet left Richmond for western Virginia, was appointed chief marshal of the fair and assigned the duties of regulating business and keeping order within the grounds.[32]

On the day of the fair, the *Richmond Enquirer*, after commenting on the "large number of visitors . . . pouring in . . . through the various avenues leading to the city," added that "[t]he stalls, extending the entire distance around an eight acre enclosure, were all filled yesterday with horses, cattle and numerous other animals useful to the farmer and connected with the interests of the state."[33] The city purchased tents for the exhibition of machinery and agricultural implements, as well as horticulture and fabrics; there was also a special display of "a statue in plaster, by W. J. Hubert [*sic*]—the Richmond artist—a copy of Houdon's inimitable statue, in the Capitol."[34] The fair proved an overwhelming success and a similar event would be held in Monroe Square each fall until 1859 when the Virginia Central Agricultural Society bought part of the old Hermitage tract farther out on Broad Street. There on fifty-eight acres of land the society developed a modern and far more commodious fairgrounds complex.[35]

City council's precipitous decision to design Monroe Square as a fairgrounds rather than as an ornamental park failed to promote the anticipated "so-

Chapter Six

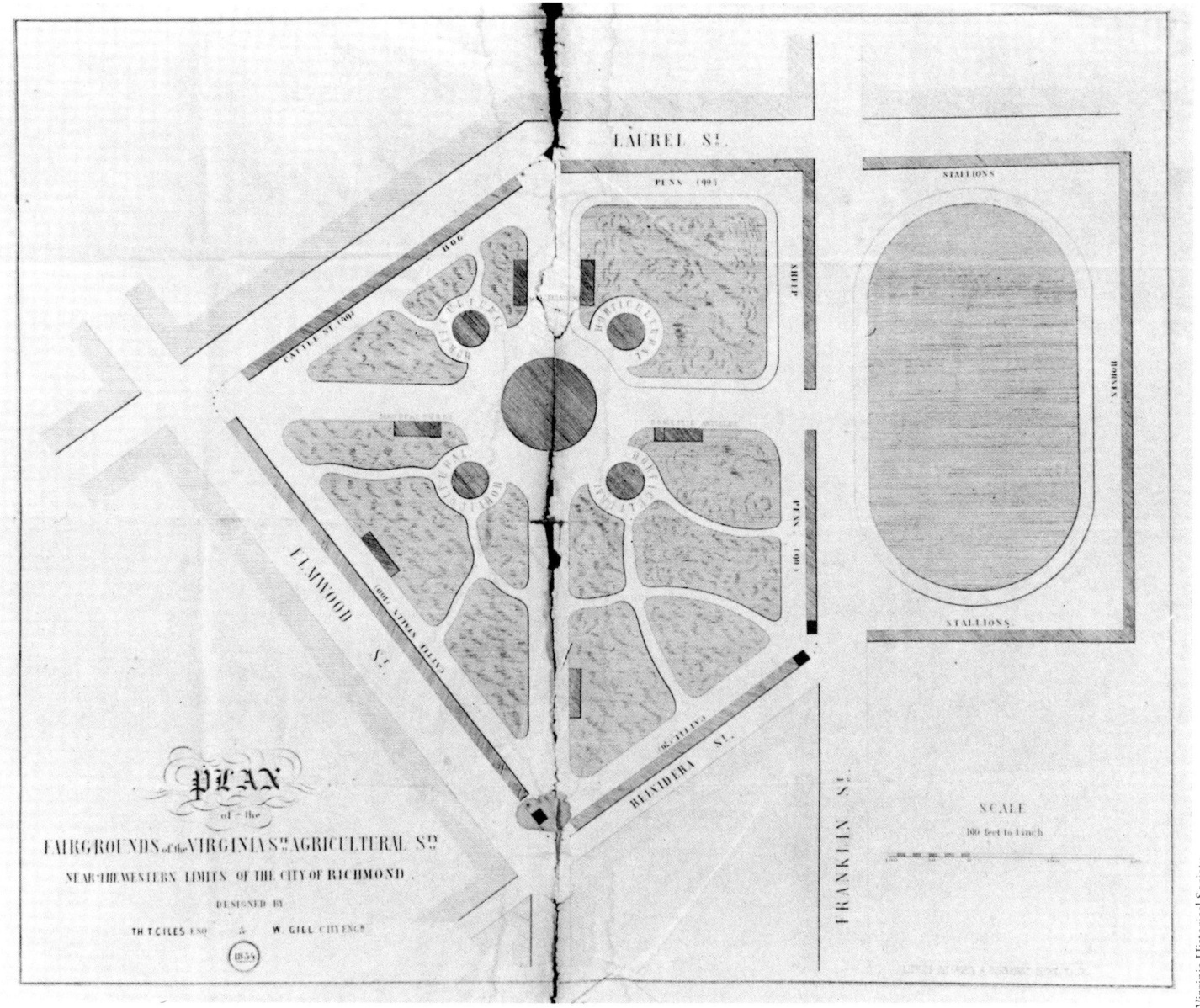

Fig. 32a This plan of the fairgrounds at Monroe Square in 1854 was created by Th. T. Giles and the City Engineer W. Gill.

Chapter Six

Fig. 32b The perspective view of Giles's and Gill's design was fanciful and probably never fully realized.

Fig. 32c Monroe Square during an agricultural fair in a print from *Frank Leslie's Illustrated Newspaper* (27 November 1858) shows a more realistic depiction.